S0-BRQ-970
Elgin Community College
Elgin, IL 60123

Praise for

"Thanks to Wolff and friends, the cyberswamp may just have become a little less murky." —*Entertainment Weekly*

"*NetGuide* is the computer world's online *TV Guide®*."—*Good Morning America*

"*NetGuide* will keep you from wandering around aimlessly on the Internet, and is full of good ideas for where to pull over."—*Forbes FYI*

"*NetGuide* is the liveliest, most readable online guide yet."—*USA Today*

"What you need to connect."—*Worth Magazine*

"*NetGuide* is the *TV Guide®* to Cyberspace!" —Louis Rossetto, publisher/editor, *Wired*

"One of the more complete, well-organized guides to online topics. From photography to the Church of Elvis, you'll find it here."—*PC Magazine*

"The best attempt yet at categorizing and organizing all the great stuff you can find out there. It's the book people keep stealing off my desk." —Joshua Quittner, *New York Newsday*

"It's changed my online life. Get this book!" —Mike Madson, "Computer Bits," Business Radio Network

"My favorite for finding the cool stuff." —*The Louisville Courier-Journal*

"*NetGuide* focuses on the most important aspect of online information—its content. You name it, it's there—from erotica to religion to politics." —Lawrence J. Magid, *San Jose Mercury News*

"Not only did all the existing Net books ignore Cyberspace's entertaining aspects, but they were process-oriented, not content-oriented. Why hadn't someone made a *TV Guide®* for the Net? Wolff recognized an opportunity for a new book, and his group wrote *NetGuide*." —Mark Frauenfelder, *Wired*

"Couch potatoes have *TV Guide®*. Now Net surfers have *NetGuide*."—*Orange County Register*

"*NetGuide* is one of the best efforts to provide a hot-spot guide to going online."—*Knoxville News-Sentinel*

"Assolutamente indispensabile!"—*L'Espresso*, Italy

"A valuable guide for anyone interested in the recreational uses of personal computers and modems."—Peter H. Lewis, *The New York Times*

"*NetGames* is a good map of the playing fields of Netdom."—*Newsweek*

"This guide to games people play in the ever-expanding Cyberspace shows you exactly where to go."—*Entertainment Weekly*

"The second book in a very good series from Wolff and Random House."—Bob Schwabach, syndicated columnist

"Hot addresses!"—*USA Weekend*

"Move over Parker Brothers and Nintendo—games are now available online. There's something in *NetGames* for everyone from crossword-puzzle addicts to Dungeons & Dragons fans."—*Reference Books Bulletin*

"Whether you're a hardened game player or a mere newbie, *NetGames* is the definitive directory for gaming on the Internet."—*.net*

"A wide and devoted following."—*The Wall Street Journal*

"*NetMoney* is a superb guide to online business and finance!"—*Hoover's Handbook of American Business*

"[*NetChat*] is...the best surfer's guide out there." —*Entertainment Weekly*

"A product line of guidebooks for explorers of the Internet."—*Inside Media*

Renner Learning Resource Center
Elgin Community College
Elgin, IL 60123

Neither *NetGuide* nor Wolff New Media LLC

In bookstores now!

NetCollege

NetCollege gives you a crash course on how to get into the college of your choice—the online way! Visit virtual campuses. Stop by cyber-admissions offices. Get some SAT practice. Sort through financial aid info online. And, soon enough, find out the good (or bad) news via email.

ISBN 0-679-77380-0
US: $19.95
Canada: $27.00
400 pages

NetStudy

Where can I get help with my algebra homework? My English paper's due tomorrow and the library's closed. I don't understand frog anatomy. From the beginne studying astronomy to the math whiz taking AP calculus, *NetStudy* can help students get an education online. Includes Internet resources for teachers and parents.

ISBN 0-679-77381-9
US: $22.00
Canada: $30.00
400 pages

NetDoctor

NetDoctor offers a powerful cure for medical ignorance— the Internet! Packed with thousands of sites that let you diagnose your own maladies and lead you to the latest research on ailments ranging from AIDS to cancer to the common cold, this is the only book you'll ever need to stay healthy.

ISBN 0-679-77173-5
US: $22.00
Canada: $30.00
400 pages

Fodor's NetTravel

Fodor's NetTravel—from Fodor's and the creators of *NetGuide* and the NetBooks Series—tells you how to find the best online travel sites. Find your way to brilliant travelogues and wonderful travel secrets—plus subway maps, restaurant and hotel guides, movie listings, and train schedules.

ISBN 0-679-77033-X
US: $22.00
Canada: $30.00
400 pages

NetMarketing

NetMarketing is the first book that spells out strategies for how corporate marketers and mom-and-pop businesses can use the Net to powerful advantage. It includes hundreds of successful Web sites, a primer for getting started, and a directory of more than 1,000 marketing sites.

ISBN 0-679-77381-9
US: $22.00
Canada: $30.00
400 pages

NetGames 2

NetGames 2 is the all-new, updated edition of the original bestseller. It covers more than 4,000 games, including *Doom*, *Marathon*, *Harpoon II*, *Myst*, and more than a hundred MUDs, MUSHes, and MOOs, plus demos, tips, and free upgrades!

ISBN 0-679-77034-8
US: $22.00
Canada: $30.00
UK: £20.49 Net
400 pages

NetJobs

NetJobs tells you how to take advantage of the Iway to land the job you've always wanted. It includes the email addresses of over 1,000 companies, special tips for '96 college grads, and a complete directory of online classifieds, help wanted, and job notice boards.

ISBN
0-679-77032-1
US: $12.95
Canada: $17.95
UK: £11.99 Net
200 pages

NetVote

NetVote is a handbook for following the '96 presidential campaign online. *NetVote* takes the user to the places where the political pros hang out. Which party does the NetGeneration align itself with? We'll let you know which cover sells better.

ISBN
0-679-77028-3
(Democratic cover)
ISBN
0-679-77067-4
(Republican cover)
US: $12.95
Canada: $17.50
200 pages

Coming soon!

Fully revised and updated, this best-seller is the essential resource for those traversing the Net for the first time and for those who already understand the limitations of search engines. With more than 10,000 reviews of Web sites written by experienced netsurfers, *NetGuide* is the essential resource for anyone taking on the Internet.
ISBN 0-679-77384-3
US: $27.95/Canada: $39.00
800 pages (10/96)

netkids

The first Internet guide written by kids—for kids! What are the best playgrounds in cyberspace? Where are the toothiest shark and dinosaur sites? How can I find a new pen pal? *NetKids* is the first comprehensive guide to age-appropriate activities for kids in cyberspace —from pirates to pop culture. Our junior Web masters rank the sites and tell us where the action is online.
ISBN 0-679-77066-6
US: $22.00 /Canada: $30.00
400 pages (9/96)

Take a virtual trip through Gotham City! Trade *Seinfeld* anecdotes. Check TV listings and search film databases. Book movie tickets online. Get up close and personal with Sharon Stone. As TV and film light up the Web, *NetScreen* is your ticket to the best seats in the house.
ISBN 0-679-77699-0
US: $22.00/Canada: $30.00
400 pages (12/96)

The ultimate guide for science fiction fanatics! *NetSci-Fi* covers topics from *Aliens* to *The X-Files*—and everything in between. Want to work on a *Battlestar Galactica* revival campaign or learn about the value of those old *Star Wars* trading cards? *NetSci-Fi* will unlock a new universe of sci-fi trivia and fandom.
ISBN 0-679-77322-3
US: $22.00 /Canada: $30.00
400 pages (9/96)

netshopping

Cybercommerce is booming and *NetShopping* will show consumers how to shop big-name retailers and mom-and-pop virtual store fronts from their home computers. Special section on the top 100 FREE products and services in cyberspace.
ISBN 0-679-77700-8
US: $22.00 /Canada: $30.00
400 pages (11/96)

How do I pick the best investments? How should I plan my retirement? How can I get yesterday's market news? *NetMoney* is your complete guide to the thousands of sites in cyberspace that are revolutionizing the way we manage our personal finances.
ISBN 0-679-77382-7
US: $22.00 /Canada: $30.00
400 pages (12/96)

To order call 1-800-NET-1133, ext. 601

Instant

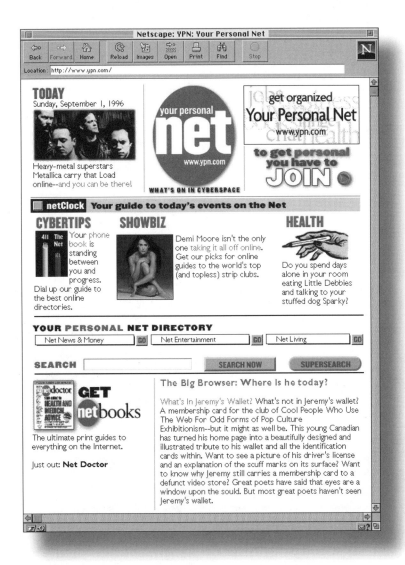

Visit our Web guide at

Updates.

Netscape: YPN: NetBooks

Back | Forward | Home | Reload | Images | Open | Print | Find | Stop

Location: http://www.ypn.com/updates/

Main Menu   Search   Browse   FAQ   Suggestions

net books

BUY the books you want, UPDATE the books you have!

"Thanks to Wolff and friends, the cyberswamp may just have become a little less murky."
— ENTERTAINMENT WEEKLY

NetBooks -- The Internet Guides That Never Go Out of Date -- will be introducing a new updating service early this summer. You can see a simulation of this service by clicking on the NetSports book cover in the bottom left corner of this page. If you would like to receive email when the service is available, send a message to webmaster@ypn.com with "UPDATE LIST" in the subject line.

NetDoctor   NetGames   NetGuide   NetMoney   NetMusic

NetTravel   NetTech   NetTrek   NetChat   NetMarketing

NetSports   NetVote   NetJobs   NetTaxes

ONLINE UPDATES GUARANTEE THAT YOUR NetBOOKS WILL ALWAYS BE CURRENT!

http://www.ypn.com

How You Can
Access the Facts and
Cover Your Tracks
Using the Internet
and Online Services

A Michael Wolff Book

For free updates visit our Web site at http://www.ypn.com

RENNER LEARNING RESOURCE CENTER
ELGIN COMMUNITY COLLEGE
ELGIN, ILLINOIS 60123

New York

384.33
Y 81

WOLFF NEW MEDIA

The NetBooks Series is published by Wolff New Media LLC, 520 Madison Avenue, 11th Floor, New York, NY 10022.

NetSpy has been wholly created and produced by Wolff New Media LLC. *NetSpy, NetCollege, NetStudy, NetDoctor, NetMarketing, NetVote, NetJobs, NetGames2, NetTravel, NetTaxes, NetMusic, NetGames, NetChat, NetMoney, NetTech, NetSports,* Your Personal Net, the Your Personal Net Logo, NetBooks, NetHead, NetSpeak, and CyberPower are trademarks of Wolff New Media LLC. The Net Logo, What's On In Cyberspace, and YPN are registered trademarks of Wolff New Media LLC. All design and production has been done by means of desktop-publishing technology. The text is set in the typefaces Garamond, customized Futura, Zapf Dingbats, Trixie, Eldorado, Century, and Champion.

Copyright © 1996 by Wolff New Media LLC

All rights reserved. No part of the contents of this book may be reproduced or transmitted in any form or by any means without the written permission of the publisher.

Published simultaneously in the U.S. and Canada by Wolff New Media LLC

0 9 8 7 6 5 4 3 2

ISBN 0-679-77029-1

The authors and publisher have used their best efforts in preparing this book. However, the authors and publisher make no warranties of any kind, express or implied, with regard to the documentation contained in this book, and specifically disclaim, without limitation, any implied warranties of merchantability and fitness for a particular purpose with respect to listings in the book, or the techniques described in the book. In no event shall the authors or publisher be responsible or liable for any loss of profit or any other commercial damages, including but not limited to special, incidental, consequential, or any other damages in connection with or arising out of furnishing, performance, or use of this book.

All of the photographs and illustrations in this book have been obtained from online sources, and have been included to demonstrate the variety of work that is available on the Net. The caption with each photograph or illustration identifies its online source. Text and images available over the Internet and other online services may be subject to copyright and other rights owned by third parties. Online availability of text and images does not imply that they may be reused without the permission of rights holders, although the Copyright Act does permit certain unauthorized reuse as fair use under 17 U.S.C. §107. Care should be taken to ensure that all necessary rights are cleared prior to reusing material distributed over the Internet and other online services. Information about reuse is available from the institutions that make their materials available online.

Trademarks

A number of entered words in which we have reason to believe trademark, service mark, or other proprietary rights may exist have been designated as such by use of initial capitalization. However, no attempt has been made to designate as trademarks or service marks all personal-computer words or terms in which proprietary rights might exist. The inclusion, exclusion, or definition of a word or term is not intended to affect, or to express any judgment on, the validity or legal status of any proprietary right which may be claimed in that word or term.

Manufactured in the United States of America.

New York

WOLFF NEW MEDIA

A Michael Wolff Book

Michael Wolff
Publisher and Editor in Chief

Kelly Maloni
Executive Editor

Ben Greenman
Creative Director

Stevan Keane
Editor

Research Editor: Kristin Miller
NetSpy Editor: Dina Gan
Production Editor: Donna Spivey

Art Director: Stephen Gullo
Associate Art Director: Eric Hoffsten
Assistant Art Director: Jay Jaffe

Associate Editors: Hylton Jolliffe, Bennett Voyles
Assistant Editors: Deborah Cohn, Rachel Greene
Staff Writers: Henry Lam, Wendy Nelson, Stephanie Overby, Wendy Phillips
Copy Editor: Sonya Donaldson
Editorial Assistants: Jennifer Levy, Vicky Tsolomytis, Eric Zelko
Production Assistant: Amy Gawronski
Interns: Keith Hays, Sam Pollack

Vice President, Marketing: Jay Sears
Advertising Director: Michael Domican
Marketing Assistants: Nicholas Bogaty, Amy Winger

Web Producer: Jonathan Bellack
Associate Directory Editor: Richard Egan
Assistant Producers: Alison Grippo, Jonathan Spooner

Systems Administrator: Jonathan Chapman
Database Technician: Toby Spinks
Administrative Director: Carol Wyatt

Wolff New Media LLC

Michael Wolff
President

Alison Anthoine
Vice President

Joseph Cohen
Chief Financial Officer

Special thanks:

Random House—Charles Levine, Terry Chisholm, Patricia Damm,
Jennifer Dowling, Susan Lawson, JoAnn Sabatino, Amy Sutton, and Charna West

NetResponse—Tom Feegel, Richard Mintz, Luis Babicek, Bob Bachle, Max Cacas, Cheryl Gnehm,
Paul Hinkle, Larry Kirk, Irene Pappas, Chris Quillian, Jonathan Rouse, Brent Sleeper, and Pete Stein

Roger Black Incorporated and the Interactive Bureau

And, as always, Aggy Aed

The editors of *NetSpy* can be reached at Wolff New Media LLC, 520 Madison Avenue, 11th Floor, New York, NY 10022, or by voice call at 212-308-8100, fax at 212-308-8837, or email at editors@ypn.com.

CONTENTS

FOREWORD

by Steve Levy, Private Investigator

When I visited the *NetSpy* team at Wolff New Media, I was prepared to be completely upfront. I would tell them that only a trained and experienced investigator can track down information on people and companies. My 16 years as a private investigator told me as much. But with a few clicks of her mouse, the senior editor soon made me realize that I had violated the investigator's most important motto: "Never Assume." A decade ago, I began specializing in commercial fraud and security consulting. *NetSpy* made me realize that leaving the traditional "retail" investigative business was a great idea.

Chastened, I decided to conduct an informal survey. I called fellow private-eyes across the country and asked them how much of their business was locating people (missing persons, witnesses, deadbeats...) and how much was conducting background checks for pre-employment, pre-nuptial, and tenant security purposes. Combined, they said anywhere between 50 percent and 90 percent, which is a lot of business. Professional private investigators charge from $35 to $125 per hour plus expenses. With *NetSpy*, you and your PC can do a great deal of the same investigative work at little or no cost.

The *NetSpy* staff could probably make a decent living by opening up a people-finding business. In fact, they are more efficient at it than I am. They actually found a death record and last known address of someone I currently have a case on—in just four minutes, without any fees!

It should be said, however, that certain investigation skills— surveillance, interviewing techniques, and access to non-public information—come only with experience and training. The verification of certain kinds of information is vital to ensure accuracy and to prevent serious mistakes. Relying solely on public records sources from the Internet may not be prudent because files may have been entered incorrectly in a database, records can be misfiled, or identical names can yield disparate information.

Still, when this book gets into the hands of clients, financial companies, banks, law firms, landlords, and others who employ private investigators for locating people and conducting background checks, there will be some drastic pay cuts in the private-eye industry. Clients will see how inexpensive and easy some of these searches are. In my opinion, if it weren't for licensing, bonding, and insurance requirements, practically anyone could set up a private investigator business with a computer, a modem, and *NetSpy*.

I've already ordered a copy for my computer-literate associate. I expect that she will soon become even more valuable to me. With *NetSpy*, she'll quickly replace the information brokers I've been paying to do these searches.

Information is power. *NetSpy* is powerful. I tried hard not to be impressed by *NetSpy*. Now, I'd like to hire the staff.

—Steve Levy
Investigations and Protective Services
(Licensed in the States of NY, NJ, FL, and CA)

INTRODUCTION

The Decade of the Cybersleuth

The 1990s is the decade of the spy. You may not have noticed, but if you look a little closer the evidence is overwhelming. Not since the 1960s, when Sean Connery saved the world on an annual basis, has espionage held us in such thrall. At the movies, Arnold Schwarzenegger recently played an "Eraser," a spy so covert, his colleagues would have to kill themselves if they found out his true identity. The fabulous '60s spy series *Mission: Impossible* was given a '90s make-over by Tom Cruise with "Check it out! I'm a spy!" gusto. There was even a new Bond movie. And every other big-screen plot involved a matter of national security. In the real world, the spy business has been equally brisk, a regular feature of nightly news reports, despite the absence of a Cold War. Former CIA director William Colby took a one-way canoe trip, and the FBI found out that the terrifying Unabomber was a hermit with a silicon chip on his shoulder. Spying has even become a prized political skill. With Nixon now a fond memory, and *Primary Colors* a bestselling *succès de scandale*, it is routinely understood that there is nothing so low that a Republican or Democrat will not stoop below it to get political dirt on his rival. And then there is the Internet.

The effect of electronically linking almost every human being to almost every other is an event of such magnitude, it will keep philosophers, technicians, and philosopher-technicians in business for ages. At a less cerebral level it means that anyone with a modem and the right skills can find out pretty much everything they need to know about everyone else. You don't have to be a private investigator to have detected that.

Maybe you just want to find a long-lost friend, look into somebody's past, dig up a company's background, or find out what somebody's said about something in a newsgroup. All you need to do is get online.

Spying is all about gathering intelligence, and intelligence is really just information. The resources in this book will provide you with new ways to access the public data that's floating around out there in the universe of information. With powerful search engines and online databases, it has never been easier or more efficient to retrieve exactly what you need to know. Once you've gathered the intelligence you need, there are scores of software programs and online tools to help you organize and analyze the data so you can complete your mission.

But as you surf the Net, you may not realize that others could be spying on you. What is unique about the Internet as a new medium is that it allows information to flow both ways—and that's exactly what makes the casual netsurfer vulnerable. Online, every time you surf, send email, or post to your favorite newsgroup, all of your actions are recorded somewhere along an electronic chain of command—easily picked up anywhere along the way. Anyone with even limited computer expertise can find out things about you that even you don't know. So if the '90s is the decade of the spy, it must also be the decade of the counterspy.

NetSpy is divided into two sections:

- Spy
- Counterspy

Spy informs you of the best places to find intelligence and how to gather it effectively. This section also gives you the resources you'll need to carry out specific missions, such as locating individuals and organizations, checking out someone's background, engaging in corporate espionage, or tracking someone across the Internet. Counterspy explains how the Internet can affect your privacy and offers step-by-step advice on how to safeguard your netsurfing using techniques involving anonymity, encryption, and preventive security.

All entries in *NetSpy* have a name, description, and address. The site name appears first in boldface, followed by the description of the site. After the description, complete address information is provided. The name of the network appears first, in red—WEB to designate the World Wide Web, AMERICA ONLINE to designate America Online, and so on. When you see an arrow (→), this means that you have another step ahead of you, such as typing a command, searching for a file, or subscribing to a mailing list. Red bullets separate multiple addresses, which indicate that the site is accessible through other networks.

If the item is a Web site, FTP site, telnet, or gopher, it will be displayed in the form of a URL, which can be typed in the command line of your Web browser. If the item is a mailing list, the address will include an email address and instructions on how to subscribe (remember—the address given is usually the subscription address; in order to post to the mailing list, you will use another address that will be emailed to you upon subscribing). Entries about newsgroups are always followed by the names of the newsgroups. In an online service address, the name of the service is followed by the "keyword" (also called "go word"). Additional steps are listed where necessary.

For those who don't yet have Internet access, here's how you can get wired and what you should do once you get there: If you've bought a computer fairly recently, it's likely that it came with everything you need. But let's assume you have only a bare-bones PC. In that case, you'll also need to get a modem, which will allow your computer to communicate over the phone. So-called 14.4 modems, which transfer data at speeds up to 14,400 bits per second (bps), are standard.

You should be able to get one for less than $100. But 28,800 bps modems are fast replacing them, and the prices are dropping rapidly. Next, you'll need a communications program to control the modem. This software will probably come free with your modem, your PC, or—if you're going to sign up somewhere—your online service. Otherwise, you can buy it off the shelf for under $25 or get a friend to download it from the Net. Finally, you'll want a telephone line (although if you plan to use the Net with any regularity, you'll probably want to consider installing a second phone line, because the cost of logging on repeatedly can mount quickly). If that's still not good enough, you can contact your local telephone utility to arrange for installation of an ISDN line, which allows data to be transmitted at even higher speeds. ISDN isn't as expensive as you might think.

To use the Net's resources—to talk on message boards, download files, read articles, view images, and listen to sounds—you need software. With the emergence of new and sophisticated software like Netscape Navigator (http://www.netscape.com), the Web looks and sounds the way its architects imagined—pictures, icons, appetizing layouts, downloadable sound clips, and even animation. Some commercial services, most notably America Online, have developed customized Web browsers for their subscribers, and CompuServe allows for access with any browser; if you subscribe to one of these services, head to the service's Internet forum for instructions on how to get on the Web. Web browsers are more than just presentation tools. Most of them allow net-surfers to see all kinds of sites through a single interface. Want to read newsgroups? Need to send email? Interested in participating in real-time chat? You can do it all with your browser. And many Internet providers, including America Online, allow subscribers to build their own Web pages, which then reside semi-permanently in cyberspace. So assemble your hardware, collect your software, get online, and get spying.

Those are the basics. Good luck in your mission—if you choose to accept it. And when you decide to investigate the Net further, neither this book nor any other Wolff New Media title will self-destruct in the next five seconds. So why not investigate the upcoming third edition of the bestselling *NetGuide,* or take a closer look at *NetStudy, NetDoctor, NetChat, NetGames, NetMoney, NetTrek, NetSports, NetTech, NetMusic, NetTaxes, Fodor's NetTravel, NetJobs, NetMarketing,* and *NetCollege.*

SPY

mission control

I. **I heard you can find anything you want on the Net. Where do I start?**

Intelligence is information—the essential tools you need to find out what you need to know.

II. **Knowledge has a price. Who do I pay for top secrets?**

Information wants to be free. Information brokers disagree.

III. **I've never seen a spy without something up his sleeve. Where do I get the goods for my bag of tricks?**

Extra gadgets to help you focus your investigations and serious spyware for heavy-duty surveillance.

What every Net spy needs to see

You were always a little curious. You read *Harriet the Spy* as a child. You spent your entire allowance on ninja comic books. You had a collection of toy decoder rings from cereal boxes. You liked to watch people when they didn't think you were watching, and you got caught a couple times. But then you got better at poking around and you found out a few things—your grandfather picks his nose, your best friend's older sister stuffs her bra, and so on. You might say you were a bit of a snoop.

Eventually, you grew up. You decided to use your powers for good instead of evil. You remained acutely observant about people and things, but you used that quality to get ahead in business. The world of work, you discovered, places a high value on finding out things that other people don't know. Whatever you decided to do for a living, whether you became a reporter or a lawyer or a marketing executive, you could still do a little sleuthing for fun and profit.

"The crux of spying is simply gathering intelligence."

With the advent of the Internet, you now have access to spying tools that were previously unimaginable. In a world that electronicaly connects almost everyone to almost everyone else, investigation is simply a matter of knowing the right techniques and using the right tools. This section introduces you to the basics of cybersleuthing.

Location: http://www.spyzone.com/CCSSZ1.html

Over 300 High-Tech Products for the man who has everything and wants to keep it.

NIGHT VISION

TRUTH PHONE

HIDDEN VIDEO

BULLET PROOF CLOTHING & VEHICLES

EXECUTIVE INVESTIGATOR KIT

BUG AND TAP DETECTORS

The Spyzone is...

Many Things to Many People.

For the security professional, government agent and world leader it is intended to be a place to learn about some of the latest technology in surveillance and counter-surveillance equipment and techniques...tools which can save lives, preserve power bases and gain significant advantages.

For the executive or private individual it offers solutions to common and difficult problems of dishonest competitors, employees and even spouses.

The anatomically correct spy comes complete with hidden video
http://www.spyzone.com

I heard you can find anything you want on the Net. Where do I start?

After watching all those reruns of *The Man from U.N.C.L.E.*, you've realized that the crux of spying is gathering intelligence—and intelligence is really just information. Knowing how to gather that information is a skill you can apply to any task or position. So even though you've given up dreams of becoming a secret agent, you can still be a secret sleuth. Maybe your missions won't be a matter of national security. Maybe they're a little more mundane, like checking the background of a company you're thinking of doing business with or finding out about the past of the person you're thinking of hiring. Maybe you just want to find someone's phone number. Now, instead of pounding the pavement and jotting down copious notes in a book, you sit at your desk and retrieve everything you need to know from your computer. Here is a list of URLs which should be included among the bookmarks of any self-respecting online spy.

CYBER-SLEUTHING

"There is a big difference between running a few computer searches and conducting investigations. The PI Business is changing but it's still growing. Just a few years ago, there were only about 4,000 licensed investigative agencies in California. Now that number is just a tad under 8,000. The types of work PI's do is changing. New areas of investigation are: Tracking Down Hackers And Criminals On The Information Highway, Computer Security And Protection, Information Security And Protection."

—from **alt.private .investigator**

Spy Links

➤ **The Investigator's Little Black Book Investigative Links** A concise index to valuable links, including phone directory search tools, investigative organizations, criminal justice sources, government agencies, and general research sites. This should be at the top of your list of bookmarks.
WEB http://www.pacificnet.net/~blackbook/links.html

➤ **Private Investigation Home Page** A hubsite to call home. Sleuths-in-the-making will find hundreds of practical sites, from how-to articles to professional associations. Private-eye wannabes can shop for an investigation school and use the Investigator's Toolkit to help them solve their first assignment. Entertaining even as it teaches you the essentials of online sleuthing.
WEB http://www.pihome.com

Search engines

➤ **All 4 One Search Machine** One search request yields results from four search engines—Alta Vista, Webcrawler, Lycos, and Yahoo—displayed in four separate windows simultaneously. For frames-capable browsers only.
WEB http://all4one.com

➤ **All-in-One Search Page** Access to 120 search engines divided into 11 different categories. Choose the news section, for example, and search through sources from CNN to the *New York Times*, all from a single Web page.
WEB http://www.albany.net/allinone

SERIOUS SPYWARE

Shop these sites for the best in spy cameras, night-vision equipment, wireless transmission gear, bomb detectors, and bugging devices.

● **I SPY**
WEB http://www.netbook.net/ispy

● **The Spy Department**
WEB http://www.canadamalls.com/spydept.html

● **Spy Depot**
WEB http://www.canadamalls.com/provider/horvath.html

● **Spy Exchange and Security Center**
WEB http://www.pimall.com/nais/e.menu.html

● **The Spy Shop**
WEB http://www.w2.com/docs2/z/spyshop.html

➤ **Beaucoup Search Engines** Multilingual access to hundreds of different search engines organized into 15 different categories. General search engines include everything from Alta Vista to Your Personal Network. The Geographically Specific category lets you link to the search engines of other countries or in foreign languages.
WEB http://pacific.discover.net/~dansyr/engines.html

➤ **Mother Load** Three different types of searches bring you closer to what you're looking for on the Net. The Insane Search lets you fill in one blank with keywords and deploy more than two dozen search engines and databases. The Web Search is a more simplified metasearch. The Mother Load Search retrieves Web direc-tories in a dozen major subject areas.
WEB http://www.cosmix.com/motherload

➤ **PIRC Reference Center** The Public Integrity Research Corporation has assembled this

◆ **Spy Shoppe**
WEB http://www.stryker
-ent.com

◆ **Spy Stuff**
WEB http://www.spystuff
.com

◆ **Spy Supply Online**
WEB http://www.veol.com
/spy_supply/spy_supply
.html

◆ **Spy vs. Spy**
WEB http://www.getset
.com/abbys/spy-vs-spy

◆ **Spyzone**
WEB http://www.spyzone
.com

Yeah, but will you pass airport security?
http://www.spyzone.com

Location http://www.getset.com/abbys/spy-vs-spy/
ABBY'S, Distributor of the
SPY vs SPY
Product Line
Counter Surveillance: CMS-Countermeasures Set
Designed for the person who wants to be able to perform most every type of countermeasures sweep with one package. The unit is contained in a custom briefcase to safely store and transport the equipment inconspicuously.
Contains:
TD-53 Advanced Transmitter Detector
P-01 Wideband RF Probe
P-02 InfraRed Probe
P-03 Line Driver
P-04 Carrier Current / Video Camera Probe
TT- 07 Tap Trap - Wiretap Detector
Headphones - Padded
Carrying Case - Instruction Manual
All necessary Cords and Adaptors.
Code:CMS-11 Price $1499.99

collection of search engines to help you research statistics, facts, statutes, and other topics.
WEB http://www.pihome.com/pirc/pircII.html

➤ **Virtual Search Sites** More than 150 of the best and most popular search engines on the Web, plus links to more Virtual hubsites containing links to hundreds more. Also features special-interest hubsites such as Virtual Tours of the U.S. Government and the Virtual World of Spies and Intelligence.
WEB http://www.dreamscape.com/frankvad/search.html

Searchable databases online
➤ **Directory of Database Services** The Poynter Institute for Media Studies has assembled this thorough list of database services that reporters (and sleuths) may find useful. Whether you're looking for bibliographic, corporate, or government information, this index lists a commercial database that will do the job.
WEB http://www.jmg.gu.se/Nora_Paul/cardirec.htm#TYPE

➤ **The Internet Sleuth** Your personal Watson for the Web. Search more than 1,500 on-line databases concerning dozens of topics from Art to Zoology. Parallel search power lets you search up to ten databases simultaneously.
WEB http://www.isleuth.com

Knowledge has a price. Who do I pay for top secrets?

Information, someone once said, wants to be free. Too bad information can't always get what it wants. It's understood that you're already paying monthly fees for Internet access, but if its highly specialized information you need, you may have to shell out a little more.

➤ **CIABASE** A historical database on the Central Intelligence Agency and the world of international espionage. Search for information on more than 100 different subjects, from the CIA's use of bribery in operations to its agents' use of sex. Software costs $199, plus registration and update fees. However, you can perform a free, simple search on this Web site's trial version of CIABASE, which contains 20 percent of its total content.
WEB http://www.webcom.com/%7Epinknoiz/covert/ciabase.html

➤ **Compuserve Database Research** Business, consumer reports, medical, real estate, and news databases are all within easy reach on this commercial service. The Knowledge Index, for example, lets you access full text or abstracts from more than 50,000 periodicals. Flat-rate access charges are $9.95 a month, including five free hours, plus $2.95 for each additional hour. Some searchable databases may cost additional hourly fees of $8 and up.
COMPUSERVE *go* reference→database research

➤ **Dialog** More than 450 databases and the full text of more than 1,100 periodicals are available on this Knight-Ridder service, which has virtually all subject areas covered. Dialoglink, its access software, costs $95 for the DOS version and $125 for Windows or Mac. Service pricing varies. It costs about $295 to register, plus access

DEATH OF THE P.I.

"Subject: Is a licensed P.I. becoming a thing of the past?"

"Makes one wonder with modern technology (the Internet & on-line databases), if the profession will be a valued service like it was in the past. Now that anyone with some intelligence can 'point and click', does one really need to hire a private investigator?"

—from **alt.private.investigator**

Wait! That was my spot!
http://eastnet.educ.ecu.edu/image
.htm

charges of $15 to $240 per hour depending on the database. You can also negotiate for a monthly flat rate.

WEBhttp://www.dialog.com/dialog/dialogl.html

▶ **LEXIS-NEXIS** If you're desperate for a raw, uncut hit of information, this is your fix. LEXIS-NEXIS offers online access to hundreds of searchable databases and features specialized information service products for the legal, business, medical, and media professions. LEXIS supplies legal data such as Shepard's Citations, legal statutes, property records, and RICO cases; MEDIS is the connection to medical info from such sources as Medline, *JAMA*, and Physician's Data Query; LEGIS is the link to Congressional bill tracking, vote reports, and campaign contributions; and NEXIS is the funnel for news and business info from more than 5,800 magazines, periodicals, and news sources, including biographies, company profiles, SEC reports, and public records. Pricing for this service varies depending on your type of usage. Flat-rate subscriptions with limited access can run as low as $100 per month. Or, hire the crackerjack LEXIS-NEXIS research team for just $6 per minute of online search time.

WEBhttp://www.lexis-nexis.com
TELNETnex.lexis-nexis.com

▶ **NameBase** A newspaper editor once called this "the closest popular equivalent to the CIA's own master computer." Public Information Research's NameBase is a specialized, cumulative index of "the names of individuals, corporations, and groups compiled from over 500 investigative

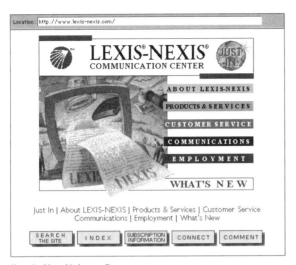

News junkies, this is your fix
http://www.lexis-nexis.com

books published since 1962, and thousands of pages from periodicals since 1973." It encompasses the international intelligence community, political elites, the U.S. foreign policy establishment, assassinations and political scandals, big business, and organized crime. You can use the program online for $30 or purchase the database on floppy disks for $79, plus $39 for updates.

WEBhttp://www.blythe.org/NameBase

▶ **Real Searches, Real Money** How much should you lay out, dollar for fact? Barbara Quint, editor of *Searcher Magazine*, addresses this question in her article at this site. Obtaining a newspaper article, patent info, or a quick fact check online can be cheap or even free—but expect to pay as much as several hundred dollars to do a thorough industry overview.

WEBhttp://www.onlineinc.com/online/online/oluser
/MayOU/quint5.html

I've never seen a spy without something up his sleeve. Where do I get the goods for my bag of tricks?

No spy suitcase would be complete without a handful of specialized and seemingly innocent accessories; the same goes for an online investigator's set of bookmarks. But while spy lore demands its agents carry cigarette packet-sized rocket launchers and blowpipe fountain pens, online gadgetry is more subtle. When building a portrait of the parties you are investigating, you need as full a picture as you can get. Use these tools to obtain background details that will add to the overall effect.

BEYOND THE SIMPLE SEARCH

"There will always be surveillance work and background checks but the days of making a living off of running simple computer searches is coming to an end. The heyday of personal injury cases seems to be closing. The new areas in legal investigation are such things as premises liability. More advanced forensic science specialties are emerging from the investigative profession such as new means if identification, forensic animation, voice prints, digital and audio/visual enhancement. The need for

Navigators

▶ **BigBook Maps** You want a tuna on rye and you want it fast. Type in your street address and the keywords "delicatessen stores." The BigBook search engine will provide you with a list of delis nearest you.
WEB http://map.bigbook.com/cgi-bin/navigator_map

▶ **How Far is It?** The quickest way to find out the distance between two points. Type in any two cities, ZIP codes, or coordinates in the world and find out how many miles (or kilometers) a crow would have to fly to travel between them.
WEB http://www.indo.com/distance

▶ **Lycos Road Map** Enter a street address and click on the button that says, "Map It!" This service will provide you with a map. You can also enter an email address and get a map of its (or at least its domain name's) location in the real world.
WEB http://www.proximus.com/lycos/index.html

Interactive - With this interactive street guide, you get access to
Atlas maps anywhere in the continental US... including some
great cities like Boston, New York, Baltimore,
Washington DC, Orlando, Detroit, Atlanta,
Indianapolis, Chicago, Houston, Dallas, Fort Worth,
Denver, Las Vegas, Los Angeles, Sacramento,
San Jose, Seattle and San Francisco!

How to get from here to there
http://www.mapquest.com

▶ **MapQuest** An interactive atlas. Type in a street address and a map of the neighborhood pops up with an X to mark the spot. The TripQuest feature provides directions for driving between any two cities in the U.S.
WEB http://www.mapquest.com

▶ **Xerox Map Search** Select any point on the globe and zoom in for a high-resolution close-up in full-color.
WEB http://pubweb.parc.xerox.com/map

Telephone operators
▶ **555-1212.com** Look up the area code for any city in the U.S. or Canada.
WEB http://www.555-1212.com/ACLOOKUP.HTML

▶ **AT&T Toll-free** A directory of AT&T's toll-free 800 numbers.
WEB http://www.att.net/dir800

▶ **Long Distance Area Decoder** What's the area code in Baltimore, Md.? Type in the city's

conducting missing persons cases above and beyond those who can not be found with first level computer searches is thriving. background checks and prescreening of all types is on the upswing. Complicated assets searches are needed as well as busines intelligence and counter-intelligence. One exciting this about this professsion seems to be, especially in the last ten years, that things keep changing in not only the way information is obtained and the way investigations are conducted, but the types of cases private investigators do."

—from **alt.private .investigator**

What's Wrong With This Picture?

Mission: Highly Improbable

Your mission—should you choose to accept it—is to search Usenet for the word, "Job," and come up with zero matches, just as Tom Cruise did, playing superspy Ethan Hunt. Pretty tough, unless the denizens of misc.jobs.offered, misc.jobs, and misc.jobs.resumes—to name a few—have put a ban on the "J" word for creative purposes. I guess that's why Cruise gets the big bucks to spy on America's most deadly enemies.

Mission: Impossible
WEB http://www.mission impossible.com

name and find out.
WEBhttp://www.xmission.com/~americom/aclookup.html

➤ **PhoNETic** Converts a telephone number into all combinations of the associated letters on the phone keypad—and vice versa.
WEBhttp://www.soc.qc.edu/phonetic

To the letter

➤**Anagram Generator** Input a word or phrase and receive a list of anagrams. "I'm spying on you" becomes "sip my onion, guy," among others. Great for writing in code.
WEBhttp://csugrad.cs.vt.edu/~eburke/anagrams.html

➤ **The WWW Acronym and Abbreviation Server** Type in an acronym and see its expansion or vice versa. The Central Intelligence Agency, for example, shares its acronym with the Cocaine Importers of America and the Culinary Institute of America.
WEBhttp://www.ucc.ie/info/net/acronyms/index.html

Package trackers

➤ **FedEx Tracking Page** Did it get there yet? Type in the airbill tracking number and find out.
WEBhttp://www.fedex.com/track_it.html

➤**UPS Tracking Page** Where the heck is my package? Type in its tracking number to locate it.
WEBhttp://www.ups.com/tracking/tracking.html

Travel trackers

➤ **Travel Time** A single link to planes, trains, and automobile travel information. Find schedule and fare info for transportation all over the world.
WEBhttp://www.vais.net/~traveltim

finding people

I'm looking for someone

I. **There are people I want to get in touch with. Where can I find out if they have email addresses?**
Directories, search engines, and FAQs to help you locate that elusive email address.

II. **Where can I get names, home and business addresses, and phone numbers?**
Scour the nation without leaving your computer.

III. **I'm looking for someone special. Where can I go?**
Reunite with your extended family, your long-lost parents, or that special someone in uniform.

IV. **I want to do it the easy way. Is there someone who will do the looking for me?**
If all else fails, professional skiptracers can help you locate the long-lost and hard to find.

I'm looking for someone

Everyone is looking for someone, but specific details can help, even in the eternal search for a life partner. For the purposes of illustrating an online manhunt, let's be really specific. Imagine you're walking to work one day and you stumble across a wounded pigeon. It reminds you of the time you and your childhood friend rescued a baby sparrow that had fallen from its nest. The two of you nursed it back to health, built a little house for it, and named it Oscar. You wonder whatever became of him (your friend, not the bird). Well, it's 15 years later and you've got the Internet and a world of people-finding search engines to help you find out. Most of them are even free.

You have no idea where in the world your friend might be, but it doesn't matter. People-finding search engines offer nationwide coverage and there are phone directories online for countries all over the world. Maybe he even has an email address. You feed his name into Yahoo! People Search and wait. But there's a problem: His name is Ralph Smith and the search retrieves more than 1,000 of them. You must narrow your search. You recall that the sparrow incident had caused little Ralphie to become an avid birdwatcher. The kids in school teased him about it (which is partly why you stopped being his friend) and they even gave him a nickname. But it was a name he wore proudly (secretly you envied his inner strength) and kept throughout high school, after which you both went your separate ways.

People can use anything as a handle for an email address, so you type Ralphie's child-

Putting hands on shoulders since 1967
http://www.skiptrace.com

hood nickname into the Four11 database and there you find him: Tweetie@aol.com. You then sign on to America Online and discover that, according to his user profile, he has become an ornithologist in Chicago and he even has his own Web page, The Birdman Online. Apparently, Ralph has become a very popular and respected professional. His home page has a section entitled, "Why I became an ornithologist," and relates the story of you, him, and the baby sparrow. You conclude that he has not developed as a person in quite the way you might have wished, and decide not to contact him after all.

There are people I want to get in touch with. Where can I find out if they have email addresses?

Sources for email address search engines are usually public sources, i.e. Usenet, so if the person you're looking for has ever posted a message onto a general newsgroup, chances are he or she can be found through the search engines in this section. Before you begin your search, refer to these sites for instruction.

Toronto: a study in perspective
http://204.I0I.3.72/livecam

▶ **Email Address-Finding Tools** A list of links to online tools that can help in your search for an email address. Includes WHOIS, finger, and Netfind services, as well as a handful of WWW white pages databases.
WEB http://twod.med.harvard.edu/labgc/roth/Email search.html

▶ **Finding an e-mail Address** According to this site, the only people who can't be found on the Internet are the Big Bad Wolf, the Wicked Witch, and the Thing Under the Bed. This Web site offers a step-by-step guide to finding someone's email address, depending on how much information you already know (What country do they live in? Do you have reason to believe they have posted to a particular newsgroup?). Thorough links guide you through every possibility from searching college directories online to badgering Internet postmasters.
WEB http://sunsite.unc.edu/~masha

▶ **How to Find People's Email Addresses FAQ** A primer on how to find people on the In-

You don't have to do all the leg work
http://www.cloud9.net/~frankp/welcome.html

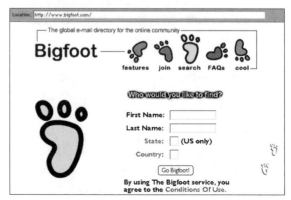

ternet. Hotlinks to popular databases and search engines are provided. Suggestions also include instructions for methods such as using the WHOIS and InterNic user directories and emailing a search inquiry to the Usenet-addresses server, listserv or bitnet hosts for mailing lists. As a last resort for finding someone's email address, the FAQ suggests calling the person (if you know the phone number) and asking for it directly. The very last resort that the FAQ recommends is posting a query on soc.net-people.

WEB http://www.qucis.queensu.ca/FAQs/email/finding.html

► Bigfoot
- Finds email addresses and, if registered, real-life locations.
- Lists email addresses "globally," but does not state total number of listings.
- Sources of listings include voluntary submissions and public sources.
- Searches by first name, last name, state, or country. Special search functions include expanded searches using nicknames, middle names, or aliases.
- Free.

WEB http://bigfoot.com

► The E-Mail Address Book
- Finds email addresses.
- Lists "thousands of email addresses worldwide..." from all online services, including AOL, Prodigy, Compuserve, and the Internet.
- Sources include voluntary submissions and Usenet.
- Searches by last name, first name, or company name and (optionally) first

name, company, city, state, or country. For special searches use "?" in place of a single letter you don't know, or "*" to match everything after the keyword.
- Free.

WEB http://www.vpm.com/emailbook

ESP

- Finds email addresses (and doesn't require a sixth sense).
- Lists more than 180,000 addresses.
- Sources include Usenet.
- Searches by full name or substring. You can select a maximum number of "hits to return," but only up to 150 email addresses. If your search retrieves more, you must limit it. Once your search is returned, ESP gives you the options of fingering or emailing the person directly.
- Free.

WEB http://www.esp.co.uk

Four11: The Internet White Pages

- Finds email addresses, Web page addresses, or telephone numbers
- Lists 6.5 million addresses and telephone numbers worldwide. (LookUP! recently merged with Four11.)
- Sources include voluntary registrations (more than 600,000), Usenet, and automatic registration via Internet service providers. Phone number database (U.S. only) comes from public sources.
- Searches by first or last name, location, old email address, or by a feature called Group Connections, which can search for certain categories—current organization, past organization, interests, past high school, past college, etc.—voluntarily entered by registered users. Smart-

Save yourself a phone call—get the Four11 online
http://www.four11.com

Name searches for common full names if a nickname is entered. With a membership upgrade, users can perform a Sleeper Search, which is a stored request that emails you when your request has been fulfilled. If your search was initially unsuccessful, Sleeper Search will keep looking automatically.

• Free "simple searches," but for the expanded search function, you must enter your own listing.
WEB http://www.four11.com

▷ Internet Address Finder

• Finds email addresses.
• Lists about four million addresses.
• Sources include Usenet and voluntary registrations.
• Searches by last name and (optionally) first name, organization name, and domain name. A reverse search lets you enter an email address and find information about the person, such as his or her organization, its address, and when the info was last updated. You can use the "*" as a wildcard.
• Free.
WEB http://www.iaf.net

SIZE MATTERS

"Comparing the Size of White Pages Databases

"It is difficult to compare the size of directories because there is no standard definition for what a 'listing' is. We recommend you use the following method to determine which database is largest: Try searching for an obscure last name for which there will be less than 100 matches, such as 'Dimitriadis.' Compare the number of search results for the different services. Try a few names to get a valid sample."

—from **Internet Address Finder**

> **Netfind**
>   • Finds email addresses.
>   • Lists an unknown number of addresses. "What is Netfind," a full explanation of the service, is located at http://www.earn.net/gnrt/netfind.html. For software updates and a discussion of the service, subscribe to the mailing list for Netfind users: email netfind-users-request@cs.colorado.edu. In the message body, type "subscribe netfind-users."
>   • Sources used include "a seed database of domains and hosts in the network."
>   • Searches by last name followed by domain keywords indicating where the person works ("to find information about Darren Hardy at the University of Colorado in Boulder, use the keywords 'hardy boulder colorado' or 'hardy boulder colorado computer science.'") Not a particularly user-friendly way to find people, Netfind works by using the finger command [for an explanation of fingering see page 88]. The service is effective only if the person you're looking for has an account on Unix computer systems that allows public access to the finger command. A list of matching do-

REACH OUT AND TOUCH SOMEONE

" i'm trying to get a hold of an exchange student that i went to high school with last year. he is from the Berlin area and his phone number is un-listed (both of his parents are teachers). i know his address but i need his phone number (he's does-n't write let-ters). the ex-change program he went through will not give out such information. what is the quickest and least expen-sive way to find out his phone num-ber. thanks for your help, kathy"

The product of a bunch of whimsical college kids
http://okra.ucr.edu/okra

Location: http://okra.ucr.edu/okra/

OKRA
net.citizen Directory Service

Department of Computer Science at the University of California Riverside

Over 5.4 million entries

Current Statistics		User Functions	Okra Info	Current Events
Database entries:	5,434,373	Add Address	About OKRA	OKRA News
Queries performed today:	4,475	Remove Address	FAQ/Help	Compare Us!
Queries performed since 9/1/95:	1,218,829	Change Address	Comments	Testimonials

mains is returned as documents; choose a document and search the names in that domain.

* Free.

WEB http://www.nova.edu/Inter-Links/netfind.html

URL gopher://ds.internic.net:4320/Inetfind

Okra net.citizen Directory Service

* Finds email addresses.
* Lists more than 5.4 million addresses.
* "Many different sources," are employed, including Usenet, voluntary registration, and public sources; submissions are screened by humans to weed out bogus info.
* Searches by any component of real names, email addresses, hostnames, or organizations, will return data that matches all or some of your search terms, and then "score" the accuracy of each match.
* Free.

WEB http://okra.ucr.edu/okra

Usenet-addresses (MIT)

* Finds email addresses.
* Lists more than four million addresses. FAQ is located at http://usenet -addresses.mit.edu/faq.html.
* Sources include Usenet postings between July 1991 and February 1996.
* Searches by given name, surname, isolated name (initials, a nickname, a pseudonym), an organization name, or arbitrary text (such as a name fragment). You can limit your search range for a maximum of 10 to 500 matches.
* Free.

WEB http://usenet-addresses.mit.edu

"Ask. If he wants you to have it, he will give it to you. Sorry to be blunt but I am skeptical when someone asks for a phone number when they already have and address. The excuse that he doesn't like to write doesn't work. If you are serious about this, send a telegram or FedEx a letter to him. It will show you are serious. Ask him to call you, collect if necessary. Now, is there a reason why you want to call him that a letter will not do, or is there a reason for him not to want to talk to you? Like most P.I.'s, we are careful on who we work for and what we do for people."

—from **Private-Eye Mailing List**

What's Wrong With This Picture?

Days of Our Virtual Lives

"Like sand through the hourglass," virtual reality has entered the realm of daytime television. And what more appropriate venue, considering that, in the world of soap operas, reality is always pretty darned virtual. On *Days of Our Lives*, Dr. Marlena Evans, recovering nicely after a harrowing stint with Satanic possession, has been kidnapped by Stefano (yes, again). That's right, the demon's been exorcised, but Dr. Evans' problems are far from over.

Fortunately, the heroic John Black is monitoring both abductor and abductee via a virtual reality visor. Little does the hi-tech spy

➤ **Worldwide Profile Registry Database**
- Finds email addresses and personal profile info.
- Lists email addresses "globally" but does not state total number of listings.
- Sources of listings include voluntary submissions of profile info.
- Searches by email address, previous email address, alias (as used in IRC chat), city or state, country, birthdate, real name, personal interests, occupation (as submitted through voluntary registration). Searches can also retrieve profiles, containing any keywords you enter.
- Free.
 WEB http://www.wizard.com/wwpr.html

What if I want to email someone at a university?

➤ **College Email Addresses FAQ** Everything you ever wanted to know about finding email addresses for anyone affiliated with a college or university, including undergraduate and graduate students, faculty, and staff. Includes specific emailing instructions for each school, a full list of college indexes on the Web, and information on how to construct probable user IDs based on the name of the person you're trying to find.
 WEB http://www.qucis.queensu.ca/FAQs/email/college.html

➤ **College Email Addresses**
- Finds email addresses for students, faculty, and staff of various colleges and universities.
- Lists email addresses of U.S. colleges but does not state total number of listings.

- Sources of listings include college email directories.
- Searches by keywords (name of college or university). Partial name is acceptable as a search term.
- Free.

WEB http://www.nova.edu/Inter-Links/cgi-bin /coll-email.pl

I'm looking for someone on AOL or CompuServe.

➤ **America Online Members** If you are a member of AOL, finding people on this commercial service is a cinch. Simply sign on and select Member Directory from the Members menu on the toolbar. Then choose "Search the Member Directory" and enter keywords (such as hobbies or a location or a person's name). A list of members and their screen names pops up. Click on the one you would like to view and a personal profile—including such voluntarily submitted info as marital status, hobbies, occupation, and even what type of computer the person uses—appears. Note, however, that AOL profiles are personally created by each member and may contain inaccurate information. If you are not a member of AOL, you can only find someone's online location if they also have a home page on the Web through AOL. The America Online Homepage on the Web provides a way for non-AOL members to find such pages. You can also try sending an email request and provide the user's real name, state, and city.

AMERICA ONLINE *keyword* member directory

WEB http://home.aol.com

EMAIL NameSearch@aol.com

know, however, that the malefactor not only knows of the goggle's existence, but is actually counter-monitoring the courageous voyeur, sending him false images through the master transmitter. Adding insult to injury, a bomb planted inside the visor is set to explode at any moment. Satanic possession aside, the citizens of Salem need a serious reality check.

Days of Our Lives
WEB http://www.spe.sony .com/Pictures/tv/days /days.html

RENNER LEARNING RESOURCE CENTER
ELGIN COMMUNITY COLLEGE
ELGIN, ILLINOIS 60123

▶ **CompuServe Members** Unlike AOL, Compuserve's Member Directory does not contain info about members' interests. If you are a Compuserve member, you can obtain the first name, last name, city, state, country, and user ID number of every Compuserve member except those who request to be excluded. However, you must know the last name and either the city, state, or country of the person you're looking for. You can retrieve a maxiumum of 30 matches, and if your search retrieves more, you will be prompted to narrow your search. If you are not a member of the commercial service, try Fourll's search engine, whose database includes Compuserve members' email addresses. Or, try http://ourworld.compuserve.com/search/search.html, where you can search Compuserve members' home pages by name, city, state, country, occupation, hobbies, or by location on a world map.

COMPUSERVE *go* directory→member directory search
WEB http://ourworld.compuserve.com/search/search.html

Where can I get names, home and business addresses, and phone numbers?

For the most part, Internet white pages databases are equivalent to what you will find in the white pages issued by the Regional Bell Operating Companies. That means that unlisted numbers will remain unlisted even online. (When Yahoo!'s People Search first became operational, unlisted numbers were inadvertantly published in its database, but those numbers have since been suppressed.) That also means that if you're looking for the phone number of someone who moved recently (about 20 percent of listed addresses change in the course of every year) and the number hasn't been published in a phone book yet, calling 411 for information will supply the number more quickly. If you don't know what city the person lives in, you can try using a white pages search engine to find out his last known number, then call the area code plus 555-1212 to find his new number (unless he's left the city, in which case, you may be out of luck). The exception to the unlisted rule, of course, is if the person you're looking for has voluntarily supplied information to a white pages database. This may seem unlikely, but you never know. You always find the thing you're searching for in the last place you would think of looking.

▶ **American Business Info Yellow Pages**
- Finds names, addresses, telephone numbers, and even credit ratings for American businesses.
- Lists 10 million businesses in the U.S., 1 million in Canada.
- Sources include yellow pages and business white pages; annual reports, 10-Ks, and other SEC info; government data; business media; postal service; bankruptcy records and legal filings.
- Searches by company name or category, city, and state special functions: results can be sorted and manipulated.
- Free with AOL.
  AMERICA ONLINE *keyword* abi

▶ **BigBook**
- Finds business names, addresses, phone numbers, and locations on a map.
- Lists 11 million U.S. businesses.

I HAVE A PHONE NUMBER, BUT...

It used to be nearly impossible to get a name and address if you only knew the phone number (the phone company either cannot or will not give out such information). But the following search engines—some of which, you should be warned, charge premium rates for the service, and only list business addresses—offer criss-cross directory functions, allowing you to type in a phone number and retrieve its matching name and address.

- **Biz*File**
  COMPUSERVE *go* bizfile
- **ProCD Select Phone**
  WEB http://www.procd.com • http://www.procd.com/pil/td/td.htm
  AMERICA ONLINE *keyword* white pages
- **SearchAmerica**
  WEB https://www.searchamerica.com
- **Yahoo! People Search**
  WEB http://www.yahoo.com/search/people

What's Wrong With This Picture?

Big Mac Attack

The aliens have been destroyed and everyone is happy—everyone except the PC-using, anti-Mac patrol who view the Powerbook's touted role in humanity's survival as a fate worse than world annihilation. Says Brian from comp.sys.mac.system: "It was really suspenseful when they took that Powerbook into orbit. At first I thought that it was the nuke since they do tend to catch fire and explode." It has even been suggested that the Mac OS *was* the virus.

Independence Day

WEB http://www.cyberbeach.net/˜rchartra/id4.htm

WEB http://www.hollywood.com/movies/independ/photo/

Let your keyboard do the walking
http://www.bigbook.com

* Sources include Database America and other suppliers of business directory info.
* Searches by business name, category, city, and state. You can search up to three choices in each field, separated by commas; limit your search by entering a ZIP code, area code, street name, or location on a map.
* Free.

WEB http://www.bigbook.com

Biz*File

* Finds business names, addresses, phone numbers, and shows how long they have been listed in the yellow pages.
* Lists 10 million businesses in the U.S., 1 million in Canada.
* Sources include American Business Information.
* Searches by company name, phone number, business type or geography. Results can be printed or downloaded.
* $.25 for each records viewed, printed, or downloaded (plus monthly CompuServe access charges).

COMPUSERVE *go* bizfile

➤ Computrace

- Finds an individual name (even if they're dead), business name, address, telephone number.
- Lists more than 140 million names in The Living Individuals File, and in the Deceased Individuals File lists more than 40 million names of people whose deaths occurred after 1928. Corporations File contains listings for more than 15 million companies in the U.S.
- Sources include white pages, publishers' mailing lists, real estate files, registered voter files, the Social Security Administration, and the Secretary of State of each jurisdiction covered.
- Searches by name, state, date of birth, and ZIP code.
- $.25 per minute of search time, beyond monthly Compuserve access charges.

  COMPUSERVE *go* trace

A shot of Georgian architecture
http://www.iarc.com/live.html

➤ ProCD Select Phone

- Finds name, address, phone, ZIP code.
- Lists more than 100 million individuals and businesses.
- Sources include "every printed directory in the United States."
- Searches by name, domain name, company name, address, city, state, ZIP code, phone number, or business SIC code. Special functions include autodialer (hotlink to actual site), business heading search, reverse search, sorting by various categories, GeoTarget (to find listings within a certain distance).
- $149.95 retail for the CD-ROM set.

  WEB http://www.procd.com • http://www.procd.com /pi/td/td.htm

  AMERICA ONLINE *keyword* white pages

► **SearchAmerica**
- Finds names, addresses, and phone numbers.
- Lists 220 million surnames, businesses, and phone numbers. Links cover 95 percent of the households and businesses in the U.S. SearchAmerica also has commercial applications for companies needing additional services such as Social Security number searches. Email commercial@searchamerica.com for more info.
- Sources include compiled databases and regional Bell companies; info is fact-checked by SearchAmerica.
- Searches by name, address, or phone number of anyone in the U.S. and automatically encrypts your online searches.
- $.35 for up to ten names; if additional names are available, they'll cost you $.25 per page of up to ten names. You must purchase at least $10 worth of searches by credit card and your search costs are deducted as you go. The first $1 worth of searches is free.

  WEB https://www.searchamerica.com

► **Switchboard**
- Finds addresses and phone numbers for people and businesses.
- Lists 90 million names, 10 million businesses.
- Sources include Database America, a demographic info compiler from whom the information is also licensed, as well as published white pages phone books and public sources. You can search by name of business or last name; and (optionally) first name, city, state. Registered users can access the personalized

THE PERSON I'M LOOKING FOR HAS MOVED

- **MetroNet** Metromail's service is one of the few that provides (fee-based) access to a national change-of-address database. It doesn't have its own home page yet, but contact information and a review of the service is provided at this site.

  WEB http://www.jmg.gu.se/Nora_Paul/cardirec.htm#Met

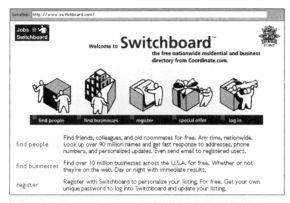

In the realm of home page iconography, Switchboard's "Log In" is king
http://www.switchboard.com

info (email address, hobbies, professional affiliations) of other registered users.

* Free.
  WEBhttp://www.switchboard.com

➤ **Telephone Directories on the Net** Links to phone directories for hundreds of businesses, organizations, colleges, and universities worldwide.
  WEBhttp://www.procd.com/hl/direct.htm

➤ **Telephone Directories on the Web** Links to dozens of online phone, fax, and business directories from Argentina to Korea to Russia to Yemen.
  WEBhttp://www.c2.org/~buttle/tel

Is there anywhere I can look up everything all at once?

➤ **All in One Search Page: People** More than a dozen ways to locate people. The search engines collected here include finger gateways, white pages databases, and email directories. Search fields are provided for each, but instructions aren't always explicit. For best results, link back to the

original home page of each search method for detailed instructions.
WEB http://www.albany.net/allinone/allluser.html #People

➤ **Finding People on the Internet** A small collection of search engines, including phone books, finger, and WHOIS functions.
WEB http://www.nova.edu/Inter-Links/phone.html

➤ **Internet Sleuth: Finding People on the Internet** An index of worldwide and regional databases to locate people's email addresses, phone numbers, and addresses. Search fields are provided, but for best results, link back to the home page of each database.
WEB http://www.intbc.com/sleuth/peop.html

➤ **InterNIC White Pages Directory Services** Provides access to Internet White Pages information using X.500, WHOIS and Netfind systems. The worldwide X.500 Directory allows users to access personnel data from thousands of participating organizations. InterNIC's WHOIS Person/Organization service allows you to search both official WHOIS servers (one for civilians, one for military) at the same time. The Netfind service enables you to find information about an Internet user based on the person's name and domain keywords.
WEB http://www.internic.net/ds/dspgwp.html

➤ **The Ultimate White Pages** Only seven search engines are collected at this site, but they could fill most of your searching needs, whether you're looking for names from phone numbers, addresses from names,

phone numbers from names, or locations of addresses on a map.
WEB http://www.angelfire.com/pages0/ultimates

> **Yahoo Individual Finders** A comprehensive index of sources that will help you locate an individual, including white pages and email databases.
WEB http://www.yahoo.com/Reference/White_Pages/Individuals

> **BigYellow**
• Finds names, addresses, and phone numbers of businesses in the U.S.
• Lists more than 16 million addresses.
• Source is NYNEX.
• Searches by state, business categories, and business name. Search multiple states, categories, or cities; displays up to 100 matches at a time.
• Free.
WEB http://s12.bigyellow.com

> **CCSO Phonebook Server Lookup**
• Finds email addresses and phone numbers.
• Lists the affiliates of more than 350 universities and organizations worldwide.
• Sources include university and organization servers.
• Searches by first and last name—in any order. Wildcards can be expressed as "*" or "?" or "[ ]." Narrow searches by using field=value (i.e. department=comput*).
• Free.
WEB http://www.uiuc.edu/cgi-bin/ph/lookup?

ADVICE FROM THE PROS

"I received a recent request to locate an individual in Middelburg, Holland. The only information I have to work with is a name and D.O.B. Anybody have any contacts/sources or suggestions for this area ?"

"I know it's a long shot, but maybe you could try http://www.switchboard.com. It's like a telephone directory... Who knows, it might work?"

—from **Private-Eye Mailing List**

Boston's Live Back Bay Cam

Sitting on the dock of Boston's Back Bay
http://shekel.document.com/cam/now.html

► **Knowbot Information Service**
- Finds email address, phone and street address.
- Lists addresses "globally" but does not state total number of listings.
- Sources of listings include the Internic White Pages (North America), MCI-mail database, RIPE White Pages (Europe), Latin American Internic, UNIX finger and WHOIS services, Quipu (X500 worldwide, by country, and by organization).
- Searches by name, organization, and country. You have a choice to search by any or all of the source databases.
- Free.

WEB http://info.cnri.reston.va.us/kis.html

► **LookupUSA** Various services are available here, including search engines for American Directory Assistance and a business Yellow Pages.
- Finds names, addresses, phone numbers, and reveals when the info was published; company profiles (names of business owners and key executives, number of employees, category of business) and credit ratings (satisfactory, good, very good).
- Lists 88 million households, 11 million businesses.
- Sources include virtually every phone book in the U.S., yellow pages, annual reports, 10-Ks, and other SEC info; federal, state, and municipal government data; magazines, newspapers, and business newsletters; verification through phone calls.
- Search by company name and state or last name and (optionally) first name,

Don't look down, Lookup
http://www.lookupusa.com

city, and state. You can use the "*" as a wildcard.
- There is no cost; company profiles cost $3.

  WEB http://www.lookupusa.com

➤ **WhoWhere?!**
- Finds email addresses, phone numbers and addresses, companies on the Net, yellow pages listings.
- Lists 90 million individuals, 10 million businesses.
- Sources of listings include white pages and yellow pages (from Switchboard).
- Searches for phone/address when last name, first name, business name, city, state; name and keywords (city, state, country, company, email provider) are entered. Searches through yellow pages by business category and/or company name, city and state. A maximum of 500 matches will be retrieved; you can tailor your search to retrieve all matches or only exact matches; service is in English, French, and Spanish.
- Free.

  WEB http://www.whowhere.com

▷ **World Email Directory**
- Finds email addresses, phone numbers and addresses for individuals and businesses; members can access the personal profiles of other members.
- Lists 12 million email addresses, 140 million business and individual phone/addresses.
- Sources of listings not available.
- Searches by any criteria (email address, last name, first name, business name, interest, etc.), in up to four different search fields, but this means that your search will retrieve anything and everything with the words you entered. Use the "*" as a wildcard; paying members get more search data returned; links to WWW Finger gateway and many other ways to search people and businesses worldwide and by geographic region.
- Free.

  WEB http://worldemail.com

▷ **Yahoo! People Search**
- Finds phone numbers and addresses, email addresses, and home pages.
- Lists addresses across the U.S. but does not state total number of listings.
- Sources of listings include Database America, a demographics company, and Four11 (for email info).
- Searches by last name and (optionally) first name, city, and state. You can also look someone up by phone number only.
- Free.

  WEB http://www.yahoo.com/search/people

You'll never know if you don't ask...
When all else fails, there are services that
have functions specifically designed to help
the desperate. The success rate may not be all
that high, but they're always worth a go.

➤ **People Finder** A unique service that allows
users to post messages describing who
they are looking for, including name, last
known address, physical description, and
the reason the user is looking for that person. Users can post to several different
categories, including Old Friends, Relatives, Loves, Strangers, Former Spouse,
Missing Persons, Veterans, Missing Persons, Reunions, and New Friends. Sort of
an *America's Most Wanted* for regular
folks, the effectiveness of the service
seems to hinge upon the probability of
whether the person being sought, or anyone who has any information leading to
them, will happen to visit this site. Despite its name, People Finder is not the
most effective method for the would-be
investigator. Perhaps its utility lies in providing an outlet for nostalgic expression,
as conveyed by this submission by Paul:
"Daphne Chick, Stranger in the Night.
Daphne and Stephanie were hitchhiking
on the Pennsylvannia turnpike. I was driving with a recently discharged Air Force
guy whose name I don't remember. We
were driving Leonard Lightborne to L.A.
We picked Daphne and Stephanie up and
traveled with them to L.A. The trip included a major breakdown in Amarillo,
TX. All in all it was a major adventure for
me, I was 16."
WEB http://www.stokesworld.com/peoplefinder/people
.html

FIND OLD CLASS-MATES

• **Alumni**
  WEB http://www.halcyon
  .com/investor/alumni.htm

• **ClassMates**
  WEB http://www.class
  mates.com

• **Reunion Hall**
  WEB http://www.xscom
  .com/reunion

• **Reunion Newsletter**
  WEB http://www.primenet
  .com/~kantoku/longitude
  /reunion.html

• **The Reunion Page**
  WEB http://205.163.65.4
  /users/stinger/reunionl
  .html

• **ReunionNet**
  WEB http://www.reunited
  .com

• **Reunions Magazine**
  WEB http://www.execpc
  .com/~reunions

• **World Alumni Page**
  WEB http://www.infophil
  .com/World/Alumni

• **Yahoo Reunions**
  WEB http://www.yahoo
  .com/Society_and
  _Culture/Reunions

Yahoo are you?
http://www.yahoo.com/search/people

➤ **The Seeker Magazine** Like the People Finder, this "magazine" publishes personal pleas for help in finding people. Categories include Generally Seeking, Relatively Seeking, Militarily Seeking, and other adverbial seekings. Curiously, the search engine scans only the text of submitted queries, so at best you will be able to find other people who are looking for the person you're looking for, too. Or perhaps you could discover that you are the object of such a search.

WEB http://www.the-seeker.com

➤ **soc.net-people** Anyone know Robert Wright? Anyone know Yvette Martinez? Kevin McBride... are you out there? The majority of the postings on this newsgroup are desperate cries for help from Internet newbies for whom hope must spring eternal. Perhaps most of their queries could be easily solved by a quick trip to any number of people-finding search engines—if only they knew where to find these search engines. Alas, hapless Tiffany writes, "Does anyone have info on accessing databases for searching for people?"

USENET soc.net-people

I'm looking for someone special. Where can I go?

The Internet has revolutionized the field of genealogical research. It's never been easier to trace your roots and locate relatives you never even knew about—including birth parents. If you're seeking someone in the military, there are several sites to help you out. These sites should get you started.

I'm looking for long-lost members of my family.

➤ **alt.genealogy** "Marrying your niece/uncle is or was legal in Italy and possibly some other countries, but it is not permitted in any of the 50 states. In about half of the states it is permissible to marry a first cousin. In the rest, a second cousin is the closest relative you are allowed to marry. Incest is usually defined as having sexual relations with someone who is in the category of relatives you are not permitted to marry. So if a couple is legally married, the relationship is not incestuous." So much for that skeleton in the closet. When the subscribers to alt.genealogy aren't worrying about incest law, they're usually asking for software help or trying to track down long-lost relatives—anyone know of Hohners in the tri-state area or Dvoraks in the Carolinas?

USENET alt.genealogy

FIND SOMEONE IN UNIFORM

- **Department of Veterans Affairs (VA)**
  WEB http://www.va.gov

- **Korean War Project: Looking For**
  WEB http://www.onramp.net/~hbarker/looking.htm

- **Military City Online**
  WEB http://www.military city.com

- **Military Information Enterprises, Inc.**
  WEB http://www.eden.com/~mie

- **soc.veterans**
  USENET soc.veterans

- **Veterans Archive**
  WEB http://home.earthlink.net/~beerborn/index.html

- **Veterans Organizations and Support Groups**
  WEB http://grunt.space.swri.edu/vetorgs.htm

- **Vietnam Veterans WWW Board**
  WEB http://www.cforc.com/gnc/vietnam/msgboard

- **WWII U.S. Veterans Website**
  WEB http://ww2.vet.org

DESPERATELY SEEKING ADVICE

"Wade wrote:
Help! Any clues
on how to find a
woman from my high
school (1980's)?
I can't find any-
thing with her
name, is there a
way to find out
 if she married
and what her new
name might be?

"Wade Wade, I know
lots about finding
people, but my
first advice is
find her parents,
or a brother with
the same last
name. If either of
them is listed in
a phone directory
in the U.S Bingo!
That's the first
and easiest. Next,
if you have an
idea that she was
married at one
time and in what
state, that's your
next step. Go to
the library, a big
one in your state,
and ask to see the
marriage files.
They're usually on
microfiche.
That'll get you
started. If you
have more prob-
lems, let me
know."

—from **soc.net**
 -people

➤ **Everton's Guide to Genealogy on the World Wide Web** The generous but grammatically rickety slogan of Everton Publishers, "Helping more people find more genealogy," accurately describes the company's Web site, which offers a number of documents for family-tree surgeons, including one entitled "20 Ways to Avoid Grief in Your Genealogical Research" (that's research grief, not personal grief). Everton's online editions of the genealogy magazine *Genealogical Helper*—the most popular publication of its kind in the world—provide a timely look at genealogical research from an Internet perspective. This site will also point you to genealogical archives and libraries on the Net, as well as Everton's extensive catalog of genealogical offerings (books, forms, software, the print version of the magazine, CD-ROMs, and more). If that isn't enough, Everton's site will also direct your online research, with annotated sections of links on U.S., international, special (adoptive, ethnic, etc.), and software resources on the Internet.
WEB http://www.everton.com

➤ **FAQ for WWW Genealogy Resources** The title of this site is a misnomer, since questions are neither asked nor answered. What is this site, then? Be patient. You'll know in a minute. A collection of links to genealogical resources on the Web, this page points to information resources as broad as the Library of Congress WWW server and the U.S. National Archives and as narrow as "A Database of Illinois Public Domain Land Sales from the first half of the 19th century."
WEB http://ftp.cac.psu.edu/~saw/FAQ.WWW.html

Frequently Asked Questions for soc.genealogy.misc Information about the soc.genealogy* newsgroups, with a description of each newsgroup in the hierarchy—soc.genealogy.benelux handles the Low Countries, soc.genealogy.jewish tracks the 12 tribes, and so on. The FAQ also includes information about the alt.genealogy newsgroup and several mailing lists, with particular emphasis on GENMSC-L. All in all, a good place for newsgroup and mailing-list info.
WEB http://ftp.cac.psu.edu/~saw/soc.genealogy.misc.html

Harbor Cam on Puget Sound
http://www.seanet.com/users/lacas/harborcam.html

Genealogy Forum Genealogical research can often seem like a lonely task. After all, who else is going to be searching for your roots? But just on the off chance that someone else knows of your long-lost ancestor or the historical progression of birth records in a particular town, you'd better stop by AOL's Genealogy Forum. Read and post messages to other genealogists on one of two message boards: the first is organized alphabetically by surname being researched; the second in terms of geography, time period, and ethnicity. Two chat areas—Ancestral Digs and Golden Gates also focus on genealogy, and you can reach them through the forum. There's also information about weekly moderated and unmoderated topic-specific chat sessions in the two areas, and sometimes there are even "lectures" about genealogical topics. The Genealogy Forum also offers downloadable computer software and software support.
AMERICA ONLINE *keyword* roots

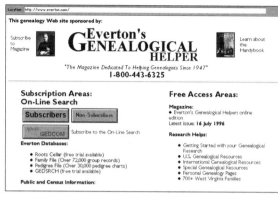

Everton's Genealogical Helper: just add ground beef
http://www.everton.com

▶**Genealogy Forum** Susan knows that her grandfather changed his name from Sornberger to Soran, and she wants to know if there's any chance she might be related to a woman named Sorrenburger she met at her health club. Antonio, who was adopted by a family named (believe it or not) Cervantes, wants a list of the oldest Spanish surnames. Ophir has some information about how Hebrew names are transliterated into English. And Lucille is curious as to whether any other countries have experienced the Ellis Island phenomenon, in which a wave of immigration wreaks onomastic havoc, altering the spellings of thousands of family names. Contribute to the discussion on these active message boards, or consult the library for software and documents pertaining to genealogical research.
COMPUSERVE*go* roots

▶**The Genealogy Home Page** An immense annotated list of genealogical resources on the Internet. Links to the soc.genealogy* newsgroups as well as to other sites. Plus pointers to genealogical research guides

and the listings of regional and specific ethnic/religious genealogy sites
WEB http://ftp.cac.psu.edu/~saw/genealogy.html

▷ **Genealogy Online** A large storehouse of genealogical information, some directly accessible here, some obtainable via links. Of particular interest are online U.S. census schedules for 1790-1890, an international calendar of genealogical events for the upcoming year, and FTP archives with surname listings, a Tiny-Tafel library, and other helpful resources for genealogical research.
WEB http://genealogy.emcee.com

▷ **Genealogy SF** Serious tools for the serious researcher, including software information and demos; general genealogical research information (including an indispensable glossary of genealogical terms); collections of genealogical data for the United States, the United Kingdom, Australia, New Zealand, Africa, Canada, France, and Russia, as well as international Jewish data; and a Tiny-Tafel Matching System, which allows genealogists to check for other people researching the same names.
WEB http://genealogy.emcee.com

▷ **GenWeb Database** For those researching their family history or wishing to interface with others of the same surname, GenWeb is a large index of genealogical databases. Organized alphabetically, each entry links to a different family name, geographic location, or ethnic group. Not all of these databases have their own Internet home pages, but many of the more common names do, and GenWeb invites

FIND YOUR PARENTS

• **Adoptees Resources Homepage**
WEB http://psy.ucsd.edu /~jhartung/adoptees.html

• **Adoption**
WEB http://www.tiac.net /users/rkytyk/KYT/A /adopt.html

• **Adoption Information Exchange**
WEB http://www.halcyon .com/adoption/exchange .html

• **AdoptioNetwork**
WEB http://www.infi.net /adopt

• **alt.adoption**
USENET alt.adoption

• **An Adoptee's Right to Know**
WEB http://www.alt.net /~waltj/shea/adopt.html

• **Cyn's Adoption Stuff**
WEB http://odin.mdacc .tmc.edu/~cyn/Adoption .HTML

you to submit your own page to their listings. Genealogy buffs might also want to look into GenWeb's sponsor, the Frontier Press Bookstore, which specializes in family-history resources.
WEB http://sillyg.doit.com/genweb

➤ **National Genealogical Society** An introduction to the National Genealogical Society and the services it provides. Read about the library holdings of this Virginia-based organization, its research service (where research assistance is available on a per-hour basis), the charts and aids available from the society, and the home-study class offered by the NGS for learning more about genealogical research. Also at this site is a selection of documents discussing genealogical research on the Internet.
WEB http://genealogy.org/NGS

➤ **PAF Review** Originally published by the Church of Jesus Christ of Latter-Day

No T-shirts here, just genes
http://ftp.cac.psu.edu/~saw/genealogy.html

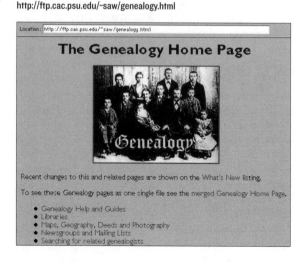

Location: http://ftp.cac.psu.edu/~saw/genealogy.html

The Genealogy Home Page

Recent changes to this and related pages are shown on the What's New listing.

To see these Genealogy pages as one single file see the merged Genealogy Home Page.

- Genealogy Help and Guides
- Libraries
- Maps, Geography, Deeds and Photography
- Newsgroups and Mailing Lists
- Searching for related genealogists

Saints, the Personal Ancestry File Review quickly became the essential computer tool for genealogists working with the Internet. Anyone using PAF will find this online newsletter comprehensive and coherent, and the links to additional shareware programs should be particularly helpful. Researchers looking to connect families via the Internet couldn't ask for a better resource.

WEB http://genealogy.emcee.com/PAF

➤ **soc.genealogy** The network of Usenet newsgroups has been described as one big family. Here, that propaganda becomes a reality. The soc.genealogy newsgroup hierarchy is sorted by region, for the most part (soc.genealogy.methods, which takes a more theoretical approach, and soc.genealogy.surnames, which functions as a sort of entry-level discussion, are the two notable exceptions). If you're Scandinavian, visit soc.genealogy.nordic. If you're Jewish, drop by soc.genealogy .jewish. If you're interested in medieval names, peruse soc.genealogy.medieval. Though there are groups for most major European ancestries—British, German, French, Scandinavian, and the trio of countries known as Benelux countries (that's Belgium, the Netherlands, and Luxembourg)—non-Europeans will have to look elsewhere, probably in the soc.culture* hierarchy. One caveat: After you choose the relevant newsgroup, you'll have to wade through hundreds of messages unaided in order to find what you're looking for.

USENET soc.genealogy

USED CARS

"I have a friend that I haven't seen in over twenty years. I knew that she used to live in Easley, SC, but I didn't know if she still did, and I didn't know her name, since she married a long time ago. I knew that her Dad used to run a used car lot, so I pulled up 'used cars' in Easley, SC, and there it was. I called the lot and asked the man that answered what her name was now. I called information and got the number. And we talked again after over twenty years. It was wonderful."

—from **WhoWhere?!**

What's Wrong With This Picture?

ID-411

Jeff Goldblum gets credit for using his Powerbook to access his ex-wife's cell-phone number in *ID4*. He couldn't have been using the ProCD database on CD-ROM because Powerbooks don't have CD-ROM drives. Not that this stopped Goldblum from trying to insert one, as David points out in comp.sys.mac .portables: "There is a scene where Jeff Goldblum has what is obviously a Powerbook. He inserts a CD-ROM disk into it (!!!) and then loads some software. Is this a preview of one of the EPIC machines or is this just one of those movie mistakes?"

Independence Day
WEB http://www.id4 .com

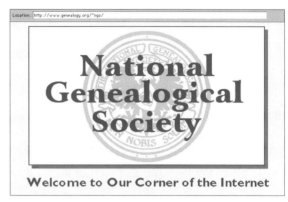

Location: http://www.genealogy.org/~ngs/

National Genealogical Society

Welcome to Our Corner of the Internet

Not to be confused with National Geographic
http://genealogy.org/NGS

▶ **soc.genealogy.computing** Computers are the greatest thing to happen to genealogy since human procreation. Read about sophisticated database programs, translators that pull names from different languages, and massive databases of public records that have everything from the deaths of medieval Frenchmen to last week's spur-of-the-moment marriage in Vegas (how embarrassing that anyone remembers that!).

USENET soc.genealogy.computing

I want to do it the easy way. Is there someone who will do the looking for me?

Maybe you're tired of letting your fingers do the walking (and the typing) and you'd rather have someone else do the looking for you. Or maybe you've tried everything online and still can't find who you're looking for. Fortunately, there are plenty of professionals who can help.

For a list, see "People Finders," Appendix I, p. 168.

background checking

I. **I want to do a little background checking, but I don't want to get in trouble with the law. What should I know before I start digging around the Net?**

In a democratic society, nothing is a secret. There are ways to find out what you need to know—and the law is on your side.

II. **Where can I find public records sources online?**

There's no need to hire a private eye when you can get the facts for free.

III. **I don't want to do a full-scale investigation. Is there anything to help me check on little things here and there?**

Sometimes the background information you need to know is very specific—online shortcuts can help you find facts fast.

IV. **I'd rather have the professionals do the legwork. Are there any background checking services online?**

Plenty of investigative agencies have set up shop on the Internet and you can order á la carte.

How do I get the skinny on someone?

So you've met someone new and you're impressed. But are they really who they say they are? Finding out is simply a matter of doing a little background research, and there are many legitimate circumstances under which you may want to do this. At one extreme you may be checking out a potential employee, and at the other you may be screening your future husband or wife. After all, it would not do to discover, as in a recent, national headline-making case, that your intended is not even of the sex you thought they were.

There are several elements of a person's background that you may want to investigate. For example, you may want to verify a Social Security number to determine if the number is valid for the person using it. A criminal history check can reveal whether the subject has ever been convicted for a felony or misdemeanor. A driver's license record generally shows violations for the past three years, although certain states maintain permanant

"Contrary to popular belief, most of the information involved in a routine background check is a matter of public record."

records of DWI (driving while intoxicated) or DUI (driving under the influence) convictions. A personal credit history reports an individual's status with creditors. You may also want to find out whether the subject did, in fact, attend the educational institution he has

Location: http://www.ameri.com/sherlock/sherlock.htm

Sherlock
It's elementary!

Locate **Missing Persons**, find **Lost Relatives**, obtain **Addresses** and **Phone Numbers** of old school friends, even **Skip Trace Dead Beat Spouces**. This is not a **Private Investigator,** but a sophisticated **Public Record** database designed to automaticly crack your case.

The Bloodhound of the Cyberbaskervilles
http://www.ameri.com/sherlock/sherlock.htm

specified or work at a certain place of employment and in what capacity. Or, for that matter, you may just want to establish that an individual actually does hold a valid professional license as claimed.

For the most part, these records are easily accessible from publicly available sources, subject to state and local laws. Keep in mind, however, that a background check, especially in the context of employment screening, usually occurs with the subject's permission.

I want to do a little background checking, but I don't want to get in trouble with the law. What should I know before I start digging around the Net?

Contrary to popular belief, most of the information involved in a routine background check is a matter of public record. At every stage of life—birth, getting a driver's license, registering to vote, marriage, divorce, death—individuals pass through government agencies and information about them is recorded.

Yes, when your third grade teacher told you that the damage you were doing to your reputation would affect you for the rest of your life, she wasn't lying. In a democratic society, government records are open to the public to ensure the "free flow of information." Many individuals, however, may consider certain aspects of public records information private. Certain states have implemented laws that restrict access to certain types of records, such as criminal or court records, but for the most part, these remain open to the public.

➣ **Fair Credit Reporting Act** You can access someone's personal credit history only if you have a legitimate business need as stipulated by the Fair Credit Reporting Act of 1971. You must also have the consent of the individual whose credit report you're requesting. At this site, the full text of the act is provided by a background-checking firm.
WEB http://www.avert.com/ref/FCRA/fcrahead.html

➣ **Freedom of Information Kit** The Electronic Frontier Foundation has compiled this convenient set of documents to help you retrieve public records. Included in the kit are instructions, a form letter, how to obtain a fee waiver, where to appeal if your request is denied, and mailing addresses of selected federal agencies.
WEB http://www.eff.org/pub/Activism/foia.kit

➣ **How YOU Can Check Out Anybody** The meat of this article is a list of government agencies you can call or write to find out public information. One must note, however, that it was written by William Sergio, the self-proclaimed "Infomercial King."

WEB http://www.paradise.net/sergiotv/art_chkout.htm
• http://sergio.directory.com/fcheck.html

➤ **Obtaining Records from Federal Agencies Using the Freedom of Information Act** How to invoke the FOIA when requesting public records from federal and state agencies. Includes the full text of the Feb. 12, 1996 act, as well as advice on how to plan and write a request, and what to do if your request is met with resistance.
WEB http://www.well.com/user/fap/foia.htm

➤ **People Finders/Public Records Databases** A primer on the concepts by Nora Paul of the Poynter Institute for Media Studies. Covers the depth of information people can find out about each other as a matter of public record and the various ways the computer databases of government agencies are made available to the public.
WEB http://www.hvu.nl/~pverweij/nora/carpeopl.htm

➤ **What is a Background Check?** The Integrity Center presents a concise definition of the

THE EMBASSY CLUB

"Does anyone know if documents at US Embassies are subject to the Freedom Of Information Act?"

"All government records, where ever they may be, are subject to the FOIA. You should know that my last FOIA request to the State Department took almost three years to process and resulted in a release of two pages with 95% of the content blacked out."

—from **Private-Eye Mailing List**

All's fair in love and espionage
http://www.avert.com/ref/FCRA/fcrahead.html

Location: http://www.avert.com/ref/FCRA/fcrahead.html

Industry Reference Material
AVERT.
Helping Employers Hire Safe, Honest, Competent Employees

Fair Credit Reporting Act

The Fair Credit Reporting Act, Public Law 91-508 as amended November 6, 1978.

Title VI-Provisions Relating to Credit Reporting Agencies

Location: http://cam.connectnet.com/cc.html

CamZone

High speed streaming video direct from your browser.

Lusk Blvd and Pacific Center Blvd, San Diego, CA

Get the license plate number of that truck—it's blocking my spot!
http://cam.connectnet.com/cc.html

IS THE GUY NEXT DOOR A KILLER?

"Too many innocent people would be hurt if arrest records were made available and the potential of abuse would be too great. There would have to be some criteria for requesting this too (ie: pre-employment, investments, etc.). The fee should also be heavy enough ($50-$100) to cover costs and make sure people aren't just running them because their nosey neighbors. (I'll probably shoot myself for that suggestion if it ever becomes fact). Without some limits, I can just see some

elements included in a routine background check, from Social Security number verifications to criminal conviction histories.
WEBhttp://www.integctr.com/Glossary.html

Where can I find public records sources online?

You could pay a private investigator to dig into an individual's background, but the information retrieved would be the same public records data that you could get for yourself at little or no cost—if you knew where to look and had time to do the legwork. The Internet is beginning to provide easier methods for gaining access to public records. But many people actually oppose the idea, so it may be a while until all government agencies' databases are online. In the meantime, there are plenty of resources to show you how to check out your neighbors (or employees or fiancé) the old-fashioned way.

Access Indiana Information Network A limited amount of public records information is available amid innumerable sources of state government information. Locate state records on abandoned property, land, driver's licenses, vehicle liens, titles, and registrations. Database searches are free with the exception of the vehicle and driver records, which cost $5.00 per search.
WEB http://www.state.in.us

CDB Infotek Locate public records from more than 1,600 databases. Sign-up fees vary widely depending on the state. For pricing information, call 1-800-427-3747 and a marketing representative will contact you, or fill out a form at this site and receive a cost schedule by email.
WEB http://www.cdb.com

Information America With brand names like Wizard, Sleuth, and Asset Locator, Information America has a variety of fee-based online search engines that can sniff out all kinds of public info from county sources nationwide. You can find personal names, addresses, telephone numbers and Social Security numbers; financial abstracts and executives' backgrounds; personal and corporate asset descriptions; bankruptcy records for all 50 states; and lawsuit filings for 40 states. Call 1-800-235-4008 for price information or email a request to infoamail@aol.com.
WEB http://www.infoam.com

Information Network of Kansas If all 50 states had services like this, private investigators would be out of business. Created

slick salesman running a whole block of people then calling each person on the street: 'Hi, I'm with the ACME Alarm Company. You need a home alarm system, why did you know your neighbor, Wilbur Jones was arrested four times for burglary? And his kid Tommy has been arrested for vandalism? Now I don't know if you have to worry about Thelma Lewis across the street, she's a hooker you know, but that crackhead boyfriend of hers, well you know those guys will steal anything to get a fix...'"

—from **Private-Eye Mailing List**

by an act of the Kansas State Legislature in 1990, INK provides a range of searchable public records databases for Kansas. In the words of one user of the service, who commented on it in the alt.revenge newsgroup, "Seems that the KS legislature set this thing up, with the idea that since it is public records, it might as well be easy to access. Cool stuff." You can search for motor vehicle and driver records, corporation status, district court records, medical boards, vital records, and much more. An annual subscription costs $50 and fees for individual searches are nominal—as little as $3.50.
WEB http://www.ink.org/ink-index.cgi

► **Public Data Corporation** Locate public records for New York—Manhattan, Queens, Kings, and Bronx counties—from as early as 1977. Includes mortgages, UCC filings, deeds, tax liens, bankruptcy records, etc. Price per search varies; email pdcmail@pdcny.com or call 212-797-9800 for more information.
WEB http://www.pdcny.com

► **Public Records Database on WESTLAW** Through this online service, you can access the Information America public records databases. Data is available by subscription only; call 1-800-336-6365 for info.
WEB http://www.westpub.com/PubRecWL/prwldocn.htm

► **RMI On-Line Information Services** Retrieve credit reports, corporate records, IC records, and more. Search fees ($5 to $500) are deducted from an account that

---

STATE RESOURCES FOR PUBLIC RECORDS

● **Cross Roads State Government** A comprehensive index of government resources on the Web for all 50 states.
WEB http://seamless.com/roadstat.html

● **State Government Link Access** Links you to all known state government Web sites.
WEB http://www.law.indiana.edu/law/v-lib/states.html

● **State Search** Links to nearly 2,000 Web pages organized by 22 state government-related topics.
WEB http://www.state.ky.us/nasire/NASIREhome.html

you prepay each month.
WEB http://www.tecs.com/rmi

▶ **Solutions Group: Private Eye Searches You Can Do** Access more than two dozen background checking services, including address finders, court docket scans, driver's license reports, and property ownership records. Subscription sign-up costs $295, plus $2.80 to $65 per search ($5 monthly minimum).
WEB http://www.vii.com/~solgroup/pi

I don't want to do a full-scale investigation. Is there anything to help me check on little things here and there?

Sometimes the background information you need to know is very specific. For information on births, marriages, deaths, or divorces, you'll need to access vital records. Criminal history records can usually be found in state

> **"Sometimes one document can yield information normally found in other sources."**

and county clerk offices. Sometimes one document can yield information normally found in other sources. For example, credit reports—which usually contain only the individual's name and any name variations, address, Social Security number, employment information, and credit history—may also include a legal record revealing details of marriage, divorce, liens, bankruptcy, and other public records.

I want to find out if my fiancé has ever been married before. Where can I find his vital records?

▶ **Kentucky Department of Health Statistics** Free searches by name for death (1911-1992), marriage (1973-1993), and divorce (1973-1993) records in the state of Kentucky, sponsored by the University of Kentucky. Perhaps other universities will follow its lead in putting public records on the Web.
WEB gopher://UKCC.uky.edu:70/Imenu%20VITALREC %2II9I/VITAL.INFO

▶ **Vital Records** A brief how-to on vital records and obtaining them from state resources.
WEB http://www.familytreemaker.com/00000825 .html

▶ **Vital Records** For less than $40 per request, this service will provide birth, death, marriage, or divorce certificates.
WEB http://www.nvi.net/search/natvit.html

▶ **Where to Write for Vital Records** In the interests of public health, MedAccess has provided thorough information on how to obtain vital records. This site's database indexes addresses, fees, and descriptions of each state's holdings, and is by far one of the most comprehensive resources of its kind. Its general instructions on how to craft a letter when requesting vital records explains what information you will need to include to retrieve birth, death, marriage, or divorce records.
WEB http://www.medaccess.com/address/vital_toc.htm

MORE THAN YOU EVER WANTED TO KNOW

Sometimes public records yield more details than you'll know what to do with:

• Birth records routinely contain the baby's name, the baby's date of birth, the mother's maiden name, and the father's full name.

• Birth records may also list the parents' birthplaces, addresses, races, occupations, and how many other children they've had.

• Marriage records not only list the couple's names and the date of the event, but sometimes also record the names and birthplaces of each individual's parents.

• Divorce records might add a list of the names of the couple's children to the record.

➤ **Where to Write for Vital Records** The downloadable file available at this site provides addresses and instructions on obtaining vital records from statistics offices in all 50 states and the District of Columbia, New York City, American Samoa, the Canal Zone, Guam, Northern Mariana Islands, Puerto Rico, and the U.S. Virgin Islands.
WEB http://ftp.cdc.gov/nchswww/w2w-all.htm

I just want to verify a Social Security number.

➤ **Social Security Administration's Quick Reference Guide for Employers** Social Security Number verification is a free service for employers through the Enumeration Verification System of the Social Security Administration. This online guide has full instructions for using the service—you'll need to send a letter on company letterhead with your employer identification number—and info on other topics such as using magnetic media for W-2 reporting.
WEB http://www.ssa.gov/employer_info/quick_ref _guide.html

➤ **Social Security Death Index** A free search by name that yields Social Security number, birth date, death date, last known residence, and where the lump sum payment was mailed.
WEB http://www.infobases.com/ssdi/query01.htm

➤ **SSN Server** A handy little Web tool that determines the origin (but not the validity) of a Social Security number. Enter a hypothetical Social Security number in the form XXX-XX-XXXX and the server will tell you its state of issue.
WEB http://www2.smart.net/mcurtis-cgi-bin/ssn.html

• Death certificates often specify where the individual will be buried and may even give the name of the individual who reported the death.

• Depending on state and local laws, driver's license records can yield all or some of the following information: full name, address, birthdate, drivers license number, date of issue, expiration date, physical description, restrictions, endorsements, organ donor status, dates and locations of any driving violations on record, drug- or alchohol-related convictions, how the defendant plead to charges, and penalties imposed.

• Plate searches can return the following: vehicle identification number (VIN), plate number, expiration date, year/make/ model/body, title number, and registration information (may include name, address, driver's license number and date of birth).

Another classic portrait from the DMV school of photography
http://www.ameri.com/dmv/dmv.htm

CHECK HIM OUT BEFORE YOU CHECK HIM IN

"Take the first step toward enhancing your personal safety and peace of mind by checking out any new person in your personal life or business. Such a 'dossier' on someone is an intelligent and useful tool for avoiding a disaster or tragedy based on a person's past actions and history. Before agreeing to meet anyone you should get their full name, age (preferably birthday), and any other information possible, e.g., license plate number, address, etc. But most important is the correct name and age which is unusually enough to build a complete dossier."

—from **How to Check Out Anybody**

▶ **Veris Social Security Number Validation Services** Provides several ways to verify Social Security numbers through desktop software, online database access, or by mail.
WEB http://www.veris-ssn.com

My daughter's new boyfriend wants to borrow my car but I want to do a quick check of his driving record first.

▷ **Drivers & Vehicle Searches** "Want to know who is parked in your assigned spot? Someone hit your vehicle, then fled the scene?" This fee-based service offers driving record, license plate record, and vehicle registration searches.
WEB http://www.docusearch.com/driver.html#plate

▷ **Driving & Motor Vehicle Histories** For fees ranging from $16 to $35, this service will perform all kinds of auto-related searches, including license plate, vehicle identification number (VIN), vehicle history, insurance claim history, and individual driver history.
WEB http://www.nvi.net/search/drivers.html

FAA Aircraft Registration Database Your golf partner is constantly bragging about his airplane. Does he really own one? Type his name into this database and find out. The data is four years old, but you can sign up to be notified when it's updated.
WEB http://www.via.net/test.html

Surf's up at Huntington Beach!
http://www.surfspot.com

The Internet DMV For nominal fees, this service will fax or email a full history of either a license plate ($35) or an individual's driver record ($20). To obtain a license plate history, input the plate number, state to search, and (for some states) class of vehicle. To obtain a driver's license history, input name, date of birth, driver's license number, license type, and state to search. For some states, you may need only a name or just the license number.
WEB http://www.ameri.com/dmv/dmv.htm

License Plate Type This document lists the code identifying the driver's type of license, from "AM" (ambulance) to "FG" (foreign government) to "PH" (physician) to "ST" (state-owned vehicle).
WEB http://www.premenos.com/standards/XI2 /index/segments/elements/ell423.html

U.S. Department of State License Plate Codes "The first letter dictates: D for Diplomat, C for Consul, S for Staff, or A for a member of the United Nations Secretariat." This document lists the two-letter codes which designate the driver's country of origin, from "AA" (Congo) to "XZ" (Australia).
WEB http://dc.isx.com/~srelan/diplomat.html

What's Wrong With This Picture?

The Net? Not

Technology has reached unprecedented proportions in Sandra Bullock's happy world of *The Net*. The Internet is connected to everything, right down to the cash register at your neighborhood drugstore. And hacking is so easy, you can do it accidentally. The online world is a playground of top secret government documents ("Damn! Who forgot to take those offline?") and hackers are attentive to personal hygiene. Suspension of disbelief, thy name is Bullock!

The Net
WEB http://www.hollywood.com/movies/bsnet

I'm going to rent out my basement to a mild-mannered young man. How do I find out about his personal credit history?

➤ **Credit Reporting Agencies** Links to home pages of credit agencies in the U.S. and overseas.
WEB http://www.teleport.com/~richh/agency.html

➤ **EZCredit** Provides software to access Equifax, Trans-Union, and TRW credit bureaus. Download a demo at this site.
WEB http://www.texramp.net/~mduplissey

➤ **IQue, Inc.** Makers of a PC program to access all three major credit information databases.
WEB http://www.ique.com

➤ **TRW Consumer Credit** Has credit reports on more than 190 million credit-active consumers in the U.S.
WEB http://www.trw.com/iss/is/isdiv.html

I want to find out if my housekeeper has a criminal past. Things have been disappearing from the house lately.

➤ **CopNet & Police Resource List** Links to official police agency home pages all over the world, from Australia to the United States. The U.S. links provide an A-to-Z index of home pages to state, county, and municipal police forces, plus access to the Crimestoppers and Most Wanted Web sites.
WEB http://police.sas.ab.ca

➤ **Criminal Record Search** For $150, Gary Ermoian Investigations will perform a criminal record search on an individual (you must know the date of birth, Social Secu-

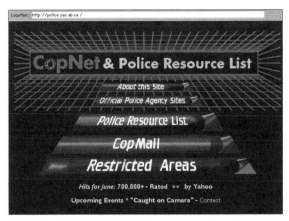

CopNet: one for the Most Wanted List
http://police.sas.ab.ca

rity number, and last known address) in three to five business days.

WEB http://www.ermoian.com/crsfrm.htm

▶ **Directory of Electronic Public Access Services to Automated Information in the U.S. Federal Courts** A directory of phone numbers and instructions on how to electronically access U.S. federal and circuit court case information. Services include the U.S. Supreme Court Electronic BBS, the U.S. Supreme Court Clerk's Automated Response System (touch-tone phone access to Supreme Court cases and bar admission information), and the Appellate BBS, PACER (direct dial-in to district and bankruptcy court computers). Most services are free or have minimal access charges. These services have generated more than six million users per year.

WEB http://www.uscourts.gov/PubAccess.html

▶ **Due Diligence** Focusing its efforts on criminal records searching, this service defines due diligence as, "the opposite of negligence." An online order form for both

Hang on! Doesn't that guy owe me money?
http://www.mostwanted.com

countywide ($24) and statewide ($38) criminal searches is provided. "What Exactly is a Criminal Record Search?" outlines what you'll get for your money and the legal restrictions involved.
WEB http://www.diligence.com/index.htm

➤ **Get Your FBI File** Spy on yourself—find out what the FBI has on you (if anything). Fill out this form at this site and send it to the FBI office near you. Mailing addresses are included.
WEB http://pages.ripco.com:8080/~glr/fbi.html

➤ **Government: Judicial Branch** All on one page, the Internet Sleuth offers full-text searching of decisions made by the U.S. Supreme Court, U.S. Courts of Appeals, and various state courts.
WEB http://www.intbc.com/sleuth/gove-ju.html

➤ **Sex Offender Registry: State of Indiana** Search databases for people who have been convicted in the state of Indiana for rape, criminal deviate conduct, child molesting, child exploitation, vicarious sexual gratification, child solicitation, child seduction, sexual misconduct with a minor, or incest.

WEB http://www.state.in.us/cji/index.html

➤ **The Stolen Web Page** Your next-door neighbor has been acquiring some new toys lately—clothes, jewelry, a new car. But when a flock of sheep began running loose in her backyard, you began to get suspicious. Refer to this page, which lists stolen property including boats, machinery, and livestock.

WEB http://www.rtt.ab.ca/rtt/personal/stolen.htm

➤ **The World's Most Wanted** You met a guy at a bar last night. You thought he looked familiar. Scan this lineup of the most infamous criminals in the world and then link to many more "most wanted" sites.

WEB http://www.mostwanted.com

I want to make sure my doctor is board-certified.

➤ **American Medical Association** There's a searchable directory of AMA members here, but you will need to get hold of a password to access it.

WEB http://www.ama-assn.org

➤ **Healthcare Locator** Is your current doctor board-certified? Where did he or she go to school? Is your hospital accredited? What kind of reputation does the nursing home you're considering for Grandpa have? What about the performance record of your HMO? To find out the answers to these questions, search the physician, hospital, nursing home, and HMO

DON'T STEAL FROM THE MAN

"If I'm not mistaken, I read that your firm offers a nationwide criminal history search for $60. Please call or email me with the details. I have the need for this search quite often and have been resorting to county searches where there are no state repositories. I activated your beeper at approx 4:05 Eastern (I thought that it was a voice number). Please respond to this as quickly as you can because I need to respond quickly to my client."

"Interesting you can offer a nationwide criminal search for $60 since there is no such database available execpt NCIC (National Crime Information Center) and that my friend is go straight to jail and do not collect $200."

—from **Private-Eye Mailing List**

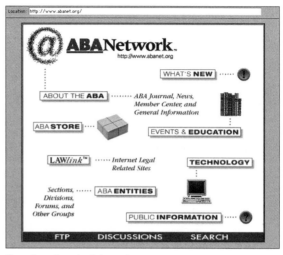

How to keep clear of ambulance chasers
http://www.abanet.org

databases at this site.
WEB http://www.medaccess.com/locator/hclocate.htm

➤ **Physician Disciplinary Boards** An index of the disciplinary divisions of each of the 50 states' medical boards. Includes where to write or call to check up on or complain about a doctor.
WEB http://www.medaccess.com/address/disc _bds.htm

➤ **Physician Licensing Boards** An index of physician licensing boards where you can write or call to check if a particular physician is licensed in your state.
WEB http://www.medaccess.com/address/lic_bds.htm

I want to check out the credentials of the lawyer I just hired.
➤ **American Bar Association** Hosts an extensive index, organized by state, for both lawyer information services and lawyer disciplinary agencies.
WEB http://www.abanet.org

➤ **West's Legal Directory** Type in the name of a lawyer or law office and view his, her, or its credentials in resumé-like form.
WEB http://www.wld.com/ldsearch.htm

I have a feeling I've been ripped off by my auto mechanic. How can I find out if he's done this before?

➤ **Better Business Bureau** The BBB brings its helpful consumer publications to the Web, offering advice on avoiding scams, resolving a dispute with a business, and more. If you're thinking of using a company's services, the BBB in your area may be able to tell you if the company has a good reputation. The bureau also offers publications for businesses.
WEB http://www.bbb.org

➤ **Consumer Reports** The online full-text version of the country's premier source of consumer information rates everything from toasters to sports cars, always with an eye toward affordability, performance, and reliability.
AMERICA ONLINE *keyword* consumer
COMPUSERVE *go* csr

➤ **Consumer World** Consumer advocate Edgar Dworsky put together this collection of links to consumer info. It's got an appropriately homemade feel, but it's well organized and even fun to use. Dworsky breaks up the long lists of links with tags indicating new items, Hot Sites," and Best Bets, speeding up the search for useful, current info. Categories include travel, bargains, news, and consumer agencies.
WEB http://www.consumerworld.org

NOT A MATCH MADE IN HEAVEN

"I had a recent case where we were contracted to do a background check on a young man. We did the usual court house visits and on line searches and discovered through in-depth checking that the subject was a 4 time convicted sex offender (females and children). The client contacted us because she was concerned about knowing a little bit about the man she was going to marry. She had planned on getting married the same month that we obtained the information. Just goes to show what can come from a simple background check."

—from **Private-Eye Mailing List**

➤ **FTC Consumer Brochures** Don't get scammed. Here's the full text of more than 100 consumer brochures issued by the Federal Trade Commission's Office of Consumer and Business Education. Find out what to do if, for example, you had plastic surgery and still look terrible.
WEB http://www.webcom.com/~lewrose/brochures.html

➤ **National Fraud Information Center** The NFIC Daily Report keeps you abreast of the latest scams and rip-offs happening over the Internet and telephone wires. The NFIC site also provides individual assistance by email or telephone.
WEB http://www.fraud.org

➤ **Netcheck Commerce Bureau** Have you had problems with a company doing business on the Internet? Search a database of company file histories at this Web site and you may find that other consumers have had the same problems, too. You can also log complaints (or compliments) here.
WEB http://www.netcheck.com

Where to get the background facts on those consumer durables
http://www.consumerworld.org

▶ **Nolo Press Self-Help Law Center** This publisher of books and software on consumer law topics presents excerpts from its products in jargon-free prose. Legal tip: Some states have "lemon" laws that apply to pets, protecting you if the lovely dachshund you just bought turns out to be terminally ill.
WEB http://www-elc.gnn.com/gnn/bus/nolo

▶ **Scams & Ripoffs** Complain about getting fleeced. The Warnings/Scams library archives Federal Trade Commission documents on a wide variety of bunco jobs.
COMPUSERVE *go* confor→Libraries *or* Messages→
Scams & Ripoffs

▶ **U.S. Consumer Products Safety Commission** The CPSC is the government agency that issues alerts when toys or other products turn out to be potentially dangerous. Check out its press releases or ask to be put on its electronic mailing list. The CPSC Publications folder has safety tips for power tools and backyard pools.
URL gopher://cpsc.gov

I'd rather have the professionals do the legwork. Are there any background checking services online?

Licensed investigative agencies have set up shop on the Internet and are offering services á la carte. Fees vary, but an individual background check can cost as little as $17. A single search request, such as a Social Security number look-up, might cost just $4.

For the list, see "Employee Screening Services," Appendix II, p. 169

CHECK YOUR POLS

• **BigFoot Congress**
WEB http://www.bigfoot.com/congress

• **Email Addresses of the U.S. Government**
WEB http://www.netrus.net/users/peace/govt_em.htm

• **FedWorld**
WEB http://www.fedworld.gov

• **Government Accounting Office**
WEB http://www.gao.gov

• **GPO Access**
WEB http://www.access.gpo.gov/su_docs/aces/aaces00l.html • http://thorplus.lib.purdue.edu/gpo

• **The Internet Sleuth— Government**
WEB http://www.intbc.com/sleuth/gove.html

• **WWW Virtual Library US Government Information Sources**
WEB http://iridium.nttc.edu/gov_res.html

IS THE FBI WATCHING YOU?

"Freedom of Information and Privacy Act Request

To:_____
_____
_____

This letter constitutes my formal request for information pur-
suant to the provisions of the Freedom of Information and Privacy Acts, 5 USC 552.
I am requesting copies of all information maintained by your
agency that pertain to myself as described below:

Full Name:
Current Address:
Social Security No.:
Date and Place of Birth:
Former Addresses (use reverse if more space needed):
Date:_____   Signature:_____

I, _____ a Notary Public in and for the
county (city) and state of _____ hereby
certify that on the ____ day of _____, 19__, before me personally appeared _____, who is known by me
to be the identical person whose name is subscribed to, and
who signed and executed the foregoing instrument. In witness
thereof, I have hereunto set my hand and official seal this
day and year above.
My commission expires:_____
Signature of Notary:_____

INSTRUCTIONS
To find out if you have an FBI (or any federal agency) file
and obtain a copy of it, fill out the above information, have
this form notarized (you must sign it in front of a notary and
provide the notary sufficient identification), and mail to the
FBI (or other agency). A request should be sent to each field
office that might have files as well as FBI Headquarters. Make
a copy of your signed and notarized form for your records.
Please note that it is a criminal offense to represent yourself as another in attempt of obtaining information.

THIS FORM IS A PUBLIC SERVICE OF GLEN L. ROBERTS"

—from **Get Your FBI File**

competitive intelligence

I. **My job keeps me very busy and I don't want to mess around. Brief me on the topic.**

Articles and organizations that will fill you in on corporate espionage in the 1990s.

II. **I need help to track my competitors. What software is available and where can I get it?**

Get these specialized business software applications and you have a corporate spy standing guard on your desktop.

III. **How do I find out about Acme, Inc. without having to ask for a company prospectus?**

Company secrets are often hidden in plain sight. All you have to know is where to look.

How do I get ahead of the competition?

You need only pick up a newspaper to know that corporate spying is big business—even if only for the makers of TV movies. And the lesson seems to be that what you don't know can hurt you. But corporate spying doesn't have to mean covert activities such as dumpster diving, wiretapping, or planting company moles. There's a legal method of acquiring other companies' secrets. It's called competitive intelligence.

"On the Net, company 'secrets' are often hidden in plain sight."

On the Internet, company "secrets" are often hidden in plain sight. All you have to know is where to look. This section will show you exactly where to find essential corporate data on the Net, how to analyze the information you uncover, and what new software—some of which is available at no cost—can help organize your research. In the end, you'll find information that's worth more than any trade secret.

My job keeps me very busy and I don't want to mess around. Brief me on the topic.

Competitive intelligence theorists liken intelligence to pointillist or impressionist painting. Close up, all you see are a random collection of individual dots or smudges. Step back, and suddenly a picture emerges. Competitive intelligence begins with tidbits

The key to corporate espionage
http://www.fuld.com/body.html

of information and as you collect them, you may not know how they'll fit into the big picture.

Briefs

▷ **Company Spies** Should the CIA be used to spy on foreign businesses in order to help American industries, such as the Big Three automakers? Perhaps the difference between economic intelligence (spying to inform U.S. government officials) and economic espionage (spying to assist private American companies) goes beyond ethical concerns. An investigative writer in Washington, D.C., outlines the debate over using the CIA as a component of political-economic warfare.
WEB http://www.mojones.com/mother_jones/MJ94 /dreyfuss.html• http://www.copi.com/articles/dreyfuss .html

▷ **Competitive Intelligence Guide** Competitive intelligence is more than just gathering bits of data. Fuld & Company presents its guide to pooling data into knowledge, turning information into coherent analysis, and distilling it into true intelligence.
WEB http://www.fuld.com/body.html

> **Competitive Intelligence Techniques** This list of links is a virtual how-to guide to do-it-yourself corporate intelligence online. Even corporate cyberbabies can follow these links to definitions and the relevant Web sites pertaining to industry information, government sources, marketing analysis, and Internet surveillance.
> **WEB** http://www.bdt.com/icemfg/techs/t0.htm

> **Electronic Eavesdropping and Industrial Espionage** Kevin Murray, a corporate security and counterespionage expert, teaches this course periodically at the John Jay College of Criminal Justice in New York. But if you hate pigeons and tourists, you can study these notes on Espionage 101 through Advanced Spying right from your home computer. Learn valuable Spy Maxims, such as "Only failed espionage gets discovered" and "The law only protects those who protect themselves."
> **WEB** http://aab.com/m101.htm

> **Free Competitive Intelligence Report** An Internet marketing company would like to help you one-up your competition in cyberspace. Fill in the blanks at this site with ten words or phrases identifying your business. NetValue will report back with up to ten Web sites that are similar to yours, an overview of its findings, and a brief outline of what it would take for your business to stand out on the Web. Use this demo as an example of the kinds of competitive intelligence work you should be doing on the Net.
> **WEB** http://netvalue.com/netvalue/form.htm

INFORMATION IS MONEY

"Prior to performing the attack, I had no knowledge of the targeted company, however to accomplish the theft of information I had to know what there was to steal. Internet library resources provided an incredible amount of information. From news databases, I was able to determine the company's top development effort which was worth billions of dollars. I was also able to learn the name of the lead researcher working on the project. There were several sto-

The Insider Threat or How I Stole $1 Billion

Espionage is easy. In this article from the Intelligence Online database, a computer security specialist details an exercise in security analysis. Using open source research (Internet resources, news databases), misrepresentation and abuse of access (false ID, posing as a temporary employee), insider hacking, and internal coordination of external accomplices (providing outside partners with remote access), he explains the ease with which he obtained more than 300 megabytes of sensitive information worth billions of dollars in trade secrets.

WEB http://www.indigo-net.com/annexes/289/winkler .htm

Using the Internet for Competitive Intelligence

Jean Graef of the Montague Institute explains the role of the Internet as a competitive intelligence resource, both as a source of information and a cost-effective method of disseminating information to decision makers. Includes links to free sources and fee-based databases.

WEB http://www.montague.com/cio.html • http://www .cio.com/CIO/cicolumn.html

Online Advisors

Corporate Security Resource Page Sponsored
by security consultants Sigma Group International, this page offers essential links to news sources such as *AP News USA Today*; information security documents like the FBI testimony at the Senate hearing on economic espionage; and other useful resources such as the CIA World Fact Book.

WEB http://chelsea.ios.com/~glenz

ries about the company's current products and the people that were involved with the development of those products. Another news story detailed a previous case of industrial espionage. The news story provided critical information to any thief. Specifically, the article details what is valuable information to a competitor and what lead to the thief being caught. This information allowed me to develop an initial target list, as well as helped me to define cautionary measures."

—from The Insider Threat or How I Stole $1 Billion

Downtown Auburn, California
http://www.neworld.net/neworld
/community/auburncam/index.html

▶ **Fuld & Co.** The clients of this competitive intelligence firm include more than half the Fortune 500. Its Web site provides plenty of guidance in developing a competitive intelligence strategy. You can email the experts at Fuld & Co. or learn about its professional services, which include research, consulting, and in-house training.
WEB http://www.fuld.com

▶ **Intelligence Online** Subscribe to this electronic edition of the *Intelligence Newsletter* to keep abreast of corporate and political intelligence matters worldwide. Read headlines for free, but if you want the whole scoop, you must open an account and pay per view ($30 for an entire issue or $1.50 per article). Those interested in Algeria's lessons for French intelligence, Scotland Yard's new serial killer–catching computer software, or Bill Clinton's new appointment to the National Security Telecommunications Advisory Committee will find this source of knowledge relatively inexpensive.
WEB http://www.indigo-net.com/intel.html

▶ **Non-Military Intelligence and CounterIntelligence** This page out of the Intelligence and Counterintelligence Home Page covers commercial intelligence, industrial espionage, security, and law enforcement. Contains links to such disparate resources as the Bodyguard Homepage and Asian Business Intelligence.
WEB http://www.kimsoft.com/kim-spy3.htm

▶ **SCIP Web Journal** The Society of Competitive Intelligence Professionals has created

Location: http://www.montague.com/scip/scipweb.html

SOCIETY OF
COMPETITIVE INTELLIGENCE
PROFESSIONALS

A GLOBAL COMMUNITY OF CI PROFESSIONALS

SCIP Web Journal

Corporate dominance is just a hop, SCIP, and a jump away
http://www.montague.com/scip/scipweb.html

this online counterpart to its Competitive Intelligence Review. Focusing on the use of the Internet in corporate intelligence-gathering activities, the SCIP Web Journal features news, events coverage, case studies, software reviews, and an ever-growing CI Hotlist.

WEB http://www.montague.com/scip/scipweb.html

I need help to track my competitors. What software is available and where can I get it?

These business software applications provide the intelligence-gathering power of a team of corporate spies right on your computer desktop. Anyone looking to stay ahead in competitive markets can tailor his online research and have it update itself every day—automatically—leaving more time to manage and strategize.

BBN PINpaper
  * Manages, organizes, and prioritizes information flowing over the Internet to create your "Personal Internet Newspaper."

ECONOMIC WARFARE

"The cold war was political. It's over. World War III is an economic war. It's here. Information is where the money is. Information theft is easy, safe, and lucrative. Eavesdropping laws are difficult to enforce. Advancements in electronics and optronics have made communications interception easy and cheap. Competition is now global. There are more competitors than ever before. Business ethics are not what they used to be. In short, the personal reputation and accountability plumb lines only stretch so far. The pressure is on as never before, and in a crowded business community the haze of anonymity cloaks many kinds of questionable practices."

—from **Electronic Eavesdropping and Industrial Espionage**

• Works with all browsers. Register at this site for service subscription details.
WEB http://www.pin.bbn.com

➤ **InfoScan**
• Manages the information that best suits your intelligence needs. Reads and filters email, newsgroups, and local and remote databases according to keywords you choose.
• Works with both Macintosh and Windows platforms. The free downloadable demo becomes fully functional for $25.
WEB http://www.machinasapiens.qc.ca/infoscanang .html

➤ **IntelAssist**
• Manages key intelligence topics, generates intelligence reports, and analyzes raw documents.
• Works with Lotus Notes. Email baker@tfg.com for pricing info. A free demo is downloadable from this site.
WEB http://www.tfg.com/html/ia.html

➤ **NetAttaché**
• Manages and delivers information from the Web that matches your research needs. Use it for news retrieval, competitive analysis, search engine automation, or as a news clipping service.
• Works with Windows 3.1, Windows 95, and Windows NT. NetAttaché Light is freeware; the second-generation NetAttaché is available as a open beta version; download both from this site.
WEB http://www.tympani.com

➤ **Netmind Free Services**
• Manages Internet information. The

products and services here include email robots, media changers, HTML and CGI script generators, calculators, and personal processors.

* Works with all browsers. All services are completely free.

WEB http://www.netmind.com

Surfbot 2.0

* Manages bookmarks and delivers Web pages to your desktop so you can read them offline.
* Works with Windows 95 or Windows NT. Costs $39.95, but you can download a free, limited-capability version from this site.

WEB http://www.surflogic.com/products.html

WebWatch 1.1

* Manages bookmarks and updates them when they change.
* Works with Windows NT, Windows 95, or Windows 3.11. Download the

For a price, **BBN PINpaper** claims to sharpen your intelligence gathering
http://www.pin.bbn.com

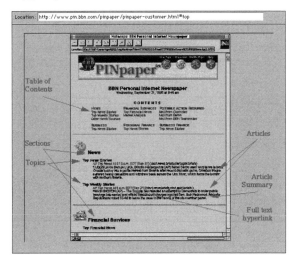

InfoScan hones in on your information target
http://www.machinasapiens.qc.ca/english/infoscanang.html

software from this site (after 30 days, you'll need to register; a single-user license is $18).

WEB http://www.surflogic.com/ww.l.x/products.html

How do I find out about Acme, Inc. without having to ask for a company prospectus?

A company may only tell you what they want you to know up front. But you don't need to look too far to find out the real deal. And subterfuge isn't necessary. It's all about finding the right source of information.

Corporate research

➤ **American Demographics** Browse the current issue of *American Demographics* magazine (currently articles on America's standard of living and the booming prison population are running); search an archive of previous issues by keyword (the archive holds articles from the past year); download a data table of "America's Hottest

Markets"; or pick up details on how to subscribe to the offline version of this demographics magazine.

WEB http://www.marketingtools.com

Watch the CNN news crew at work
http://www.cnn.com/EVENTS
/inhouse_camera/index.html

Biz*List U.S. and Canadian business info at your fingertips 24/7 (except for 3 hours a month when the database is updated). Compuserve's Biz*List contains data from the American Business Information database, including company names, addresses, phone numbers, names of executives, SIC codes, number pf employees, estimated sales volume, credit rating codes, and much more. Search by name, industry category, or geographic area. In addition to Compuserve access charges, use of this service costs $.35 per full record viewed, printed, or downloaded.

COMPUSERVE*go* bizlist

Business Demographics Two searches are available to help business analyze their markets. Select a geographic area to analyze by ZIP code, country, city, state, ADI (Arbitron TV market), or DMA (Nielsen TV market). The Business-to-Business Report provides the total number of employees in each Standard Industrial Classification (SIC) category for that area. The Advertisers' Service Report limits data to the retail trade. There is a fee of $10 per search, in addition to Compuserve monthly access charges.

COMPUSERVE*go* busdem

Business Wire: Company News on the Net
Business Wire allows you to search for the latest corporate press releases organized by company name. Links to corpo-

rate Web sites are also included, where appropriate. Companies obviously try to put the best possible spin on things in press releases, so for a more complete (if jargon-laden) account of what's going on, check corporate filings in the Securities & Exchange Commission's EDGAR database.

WEB http://www.businesswire.com/cnn

➤ **Company Research** Know your key competitors inside and out with the help of this site, which provides company news, in-depth spotlight features on specific companies, and Company Profiles that list the intimate details of hundreds of companies (from basic company overviews to the names of their mailroom personnel). On the message boards, there is a section called Company Research which contains more company profiles, targeted stock reports, financial statements, earnings and estimates info, and more.

AMERICA ONLINE *keyword* company research

➤ **Corporate Financials Online** CFO presents press releases from a few dozen public companies on its own Web site, with news of earnings, staff changes, and so on. The latest releases are posted soon after they're sent to the major news outlets. The site also includes links to the corporate-announcement pages of major companies like Apple, Boeing, Kodak, and Motorola.

WEB http://www.cfonews.com

➤ **Dun & Bradstreet Security Checks** Get a background report on a U.S. company for $20. Find out about a company's history,

---

IMPROVE YOUR TECHNIQUE

"The question is... who monitors or cares about this company? The basic sources of company information are databases; directories; newspapers; newsletters; libraries; government and the Internet. The government, for example has a multitude of regulatory agencies at all levels which collect information on all types of companies. They monitor firms in order to protect workers, consumers, stockholders and the environment. A company generally will disclose vital plant and product-level intelligence through these regulatory filings. By regulations... city, state, and federal agencies, or other legislative bodies may be very interested in this company due to their regulatory mission and maintain records of complaints, in-operations, management, special events, and recent news.

WEB http://www.dbisna.com/dbis/product/secure.htm

➤ **EDGAR Online** A subscription service (not affiliated with the SEC) that gives you more timely access to EDGAR filings than the free site. You can set up a "WatchList" to monitor certain companies so that the service will send you an email whenever they submit a new filing.

WEB http://www.edgar-online.com

➤ **Hoover's Business Profiles** Search the full text of Hoover's Handbook for detailed profiles of nearly 2,000 of the largest and fastest-growing public and private companies in the U.S. and the world. Profiles are exhaustive with info that includes assets, sales figures, number of employees, CEO and CFO salaries, and company products. In addition, the profiles feature long and gossipy descriptions of a company's history and culture. You can use the profiles to get the location of a company's office, its future goals and ongoing programs, and its recent stock prices, plus phone, address, and fax information. The

vestigations, filings, and applications by the firm. Also by geography... a region or local community may consider a company, and its product lines or business units very important. Try the local Chamber of Commerce... for general information about the company in relation to the area. Or, newspaper reporters... for articles and first-hand knowledge about the company. Or, by industry... a company may be closely monitored by trade unions and associations... for work conditions, opinions and rankings of the company. Another source are suppliers... for information and opinions about the company you are assessing. Tip... use a phone directory to obtain the contact numbers of some of these sources."

—from **Competitive Intelligence Techniques**

Information isn't free, but it's pretty cheap
http://www.dbisna.com/dbis/product/secure.htm

Location: http://www.dbisna.com/dbis/product/secure.htm

| online access | news, views and trends | business how-to's | your company and D&B | product catalog | D&B's sites worldwide |

Welcome to D&B's Online Access for the Business Background Report

Use your secure browser to search D&B's vast database of more than 10 million U.S. companies. There's no charge for searching -- you pay only when you order a report.

The **Business Background Report** provides useful information on a U.S. company's history and operations, business background of its management, special events and recent newsworthy items D&B has learned of -- for just **$20.00 (U.S.)** per report.

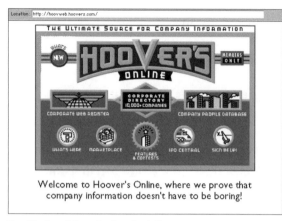

Welcome to Hoover's Online, where we prove that company information doesn't have to be boring!

Sound business information doesn't exist in a vacuum
http://www.hoovweb.hoovers.com

exhaustive resources at Hoover's Business Profiles will help you get to know the market one company at a time. Note: To search the database on the Web, you have to subscribe at a cost of $9.95 per month.

AMERICA ONLINE *keyword* **hoover**

COMPUSERVE *go* **hoover**

WEB http://www.hoovweb.hoovers.com

➤ **Hoover's Industry Profiles** Facts and figures on nearly 200 U.S. industries ranging from construction to health care to transportation. The comprehensive list includes 30 service and 150 manufacturing industries. Filled with projections, trend analysis, and statistics from American companies (supplies, expenditures, employee numbers), the reports are long and detailed. If you want a quick but smart rundown of issues and challenges facing an industry for your market analysis, the reports spell those out well.

AMERICA ONLINE *keyword* **industry profiles**

➤ **I/spy Internet News Search** News and stock analysis are the specialties at this metasearch engine. Type in a master search phrase and your keywords will be loaded into search forms for dozens of different sources, from CNN to the SEC to the Wall Street Journal. You decide which search engines you want to access without having to link to them.
WEB http://www.oneworld.net/ispy

Just another today in Tokyo
http://www.laterra.or.jp/today
/today_e.html

➤ **IBM InfoMarket** Access 6,300 journals, 770 newsletters, 300 newspapers, 66 news-wires, and information on 11 million companies. Corporate users must register to open an account for this fee-based service.
WEB http://www.infomkt.ibm.com

➤ **Industry.Net** Check out Industry.Net Report for news and corporate press releases organized by field: business, manufacturing, and computing. The main draw is an online mall where manufacturing and wholesaling companies sell their products.
WEB http://www.industry.net

➤ **infoMCI: Extra! Extra!** Tracking a specific sector in the market? Keep up with the latest with these short news stories from Reuters, broken down into such industry categories as retailing, telecommunications, health care, and financial services. The site also has top business and general-news headlines updated three times a day.
WEB http://www.fyionline.com/infoMCI

➤ **Investor In Touch** Contains a useful directory of more than 15,000 public companies worldwide that are tracked by financial analysts. Big blue-chip companies often have dozens of analysts following their stock, while lesser-known or less-interesting companies might have none. The database gives earnings estimates from the analysts and lets you know which analysts follow a particular stock. A handy tool for careful stock-pickers.

WEB http://www.money.com/ssnhome.html

Patent Search Does your corporate archrival already have a patent on your brilliant idea? Search by class, subclass, or patent numbers, and retrieve patent titles or abstracts. This page also contains an index and manual of classification, the text of federal patent laws, an archive of stories from the Internet Patent News Service, and a shopping mall of patent services.

WEB http://sunsite.unc.edu/patents/intropat.html

PR Newswire: Company News On Call A wire service that distributes press releases from public and private companies to the news media. Companies often make major announcements and release their earnings reports through PR Newswire and/or Business Wire, a competing service. PR Newswire's Web site lets you look up press releases filed by company name.

WEB http://www.prnewswire.com/cnoc.html

S&P Online For a fee, this service distills the recent business histories of more than 5,000 companies to bring you essential information, including recent market activity, dividend info, product line summaries, and earning estimates.

COMPUSERVE *go* s&p

THE FRENCH, SPIES, & COPYRIGHTS

"Once again the exciting world of being a spy intrudes into the world of patenting. Last time it was spying for the Justice Department (against companies using patents to create monopolies). This time it involves patents, copyrights and France. At the end of this message you will hear a beep — take the bits of this secret message and eat them Last week France's state-owned computer company, Groupe Bull, announced that last October it had filed a copyright infringement lawsuit against Texas Instruments. The case involves smart card microprocessor technology that is copyrighted by Groupe Bull in 1983. The

▶ **SEC EDGAR Database** The single most comprehensive and detailed source of company information on the Internet, and amazingly enough, it's free. Public companies are required to file certain documents disclosing their financial position and business activities with the Securities & Exchange Commission on a regular basis. Most companies now submit these documents electronically, and the SEC files all of them in the EDGAR database. The database goes back to 1994, and the documents are available online within one or two days of submission. Some careful reading and a little knowledge of how a balance sheet works can turn up some valuable insights in this mountain of information. Because companies are required to tell the SEC about lawsuits they're involved in or threats to their business, recent SEC filings should be a must-read for anyone considering a major investment in a company's stock.

WEB http://www.sec.gov/edgarhp.htm

▶ **Silicon Investor** An amazingly useful site devoted to investment in high-tech stocks. Because of the fast-changing nature of the electronics and computer industries, these stocks tend to fluctuate wildly. Investors who go for this sector are the kind who can tolerate a little whiplash. A few thousand of those investors have found their way to this page, where they debate chart patterns and arcane technological advancements with gusto. The graphs offered are perhaps the most attractive and useful ones on the Web. A must-see for high-tech fans.

WEB http://www.techstocks.com/investor

suit was filed in US District Court in Virginia, but has been transferred to Texas. But, according to an article in L'-Express, Texas Instruments is fighting back with allegations that the technology Bull claims to have developed was based on technology stolen from Texas Instruments during a French industrial espionage action that allegedly was uncovered by US authorities in 1980. Naturally, Bull denies any connection to industrial-espionage activity by French agents. I'm skeptical, since what's the point of being owned by a government if fellow government agencies (like the spies) don't supply you with information they find for that very purpose?"

—from **Patent Search**

Where captains of industry can catch wind of the latest news
http://www.indusrty.com

> **Supersite** Demographics reports in a matter of minutes. Tailor your search to deliver the data you need to know, including population, age, income, and housing stats for any geographic area or market definition. Fees range from $25 to $45 per specialized report, plus CompuServe monthly fees. Choose from demographics, purchase potential, or target marketing reports.
>
> COMPUSERVE *go* supersite

Business credit reports services
For a listing, see "Credit Report Services," Appendix IV, p. 175.

Corporate spies for hire
For a listing, see "Corporate Spies for Hire," Appendix V, p. 176.

surf-watching

I. How do I find out if someone is online right now?

Put the finger on someone or locate a member of AOL.

II. What do I have to do to find out if someone's posted to a newsgroup?

Easy-to-use search engines archive Usenet for your viewing pleasure.

III. How can I find out where someone has been surfing online?

All the tracking, monitoring, filtering, and blocking software you'll ever need.

I want to see what other folks are up to online

Remember your childhood best friend's older sister? The one who used to enhance her cleavage with Kleenex? Your nostalgia piqued, you could input her name into the DejaNews newsgroup search engine and see if she's posted to alt.clothing.lingerie lately. Then again, you may have better reasons for checking someone out online. You might be an employer who believes that your workers are spending too much time in the chat rooms on CompuServe. Or maybe you're a parent genuinely concerned that junior might stray into areas where inappropriate material is the order of the day. Or perhaps you run a Web site and you'd like to know where visitors are traveling within it. Whatever your reasons for monitoring online activity, you can use the Internet to access an abundance of resources and software that will satisfy your surveillance needs.

How do I find out if someone is online right now?

Net terminology tells us that it is possible to finger someone online. (And once those of you at the back stop tittering we can proceed.) The technique has been around for some time, but it is no longer as reliable as it used to be. Theoretically, you can use the finger command to retrieve information about people or groups all over the Internet. Depending on the system, the finger command can display your target's login name, full name, office location and phone, login

Get in touch with someone
http://www.interlink.no/finger

time, idle time, time mail was last read, default shell, when your target was last logged on, and the target's ˜/.plan and ˜/.project files.
However fingering only works if the target's

> **"Net terminology tells us that it's possible to finger someone online."**

Internet host is running a finger server, and some systems don't host accounts for privacy reasons. Fingering will usually work for email addresses ending in .org, .net, or .edu, but usually not .com.

The bit of information about the "time/date of last login" is no longer a good indicator of when the person fingered last used the account because most people access email using a desktop program without ever logging in to their shell accounts. So even if your target has been checking email every day, his finger file might lead you to believe he hasn't logged on for months.

Plan files are text files of any length that contain whatever information a person wants to include, which may be anything from an office phone number and address to the names of their children and pets. These days, however, some machines only allow people in the same system to access each other's plans. Here are a few guides to the art of fingering:

➤ **Finger!** Defines the activity with complete instructions for doing it from your desktop (using Macintosh, Windows' WsFinger or WsFinger95, or Eudora), Unix, Vax shell, or the Web. Links included. WEB http://www.amherst.edu/~atstarr/computers/finger.html

➤ **Finger FAQ** This section of the larger FAQ on Signature, Fingers, and Customized Headers details instructions for the Unix finger command, fingering with a Web browser, and fingering yourself. WEB http://www.smartpages.com/faqs/signature_finger_faq/faq-doc-22.html

UNCLE SAM AND THE NET...

"...folks, In the days we are in of 'Uncle Sam' wanting to control the internet, an obvious question comes to mind. For whatever reason, suppose uncle sam wants to monitor the internet use of a person. What would be the easiest way to do this? Is there software out there for monitoring and documenting internet use of a given computer address? just curious about the state of things."

"In the recent Argentine case we saw DOJ mention of an item called "I-watch" and we can assume quite a bit

Straight up, no salt for the virtual drinkers of AOL
America Online *keyword* Control + F

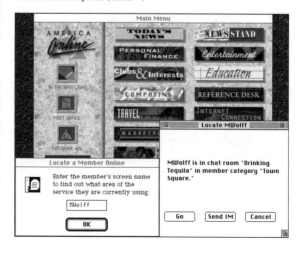

➤ **Fingering Thru the Web** A brief how-to on fingering without having to depend on bandwidth-wasting finger gateways.
WEB http://www.ling.nwu.edu/~sburke/html/finger.html

Basic Finger Gateways
➤ **Brett's WWW Finger Gateway**
WEB http://cei.haag.umkc.edu/people/brett/finger.html

➤ **Doug's WWW Finger Gateway**
WEB http://www-bprc.mps.ohio-state.edu/cgi-bin /finger.pl

➤ **Finger Gateway at Digital CRL**
WEB http://www.crl.dec.com/cgi-bin/finger

➤ **Finger Gateway at InterLink AS**
WEB http://www.interlink.no/finger

➤ **Finger Gateway at MIT**
WEB http://www.mit.edu/finger

Finger Gateways with Added Features
➤ **Finger Gateway with Faces** Supports user-submitted picon-images for faces.
WEB http://www.cs.indiana.edu/finger/gateway

➤ **HyperFinger** A finger gateway with options to limit finger info you're looking for.
WEB http://www.middlebury.edu/~otisg/cgi /HyperFinger.cgi

On the Commercial Services
➤ **America Online** From the menu bar, select "Locate a Member Online" (control F), then type in the member's screen name— a screen will tell you whether or not the member is online and if so, what service area the member is using.
AMERICA ONLINE *keyword* **Control + F**

of work is being done on this type of information gathering tool. Though similar to newsbots and such I think most monitoring will follow the standards already set for government use of evidence. What I am refering to is the serving of a warrant on an ISP and the goverment using monitoring tools at that point to capture the actions of a suspect. I'd say most ISP's would already have some form of maintenance tool that would allow for capturing data. My guess is the link would be provided by the ISP and the investigating agency would use its own hardware and software."

—from **comp .security.misc**

What do I have to do to find out if someone's posted to a newsgroup?

Some of the large search engines, such as Alta Vista and Excite, enable you to search Usenet postings by keyword, but a few, specialized search engines can save you time by letting you tailor and filter your search requests according to your specific needs.

➤ **Internet Sleuth: Usenet News** A collection of engines that search Usenet in some form or another. Input your target's name and see what kind of messages he or she has been posting lately.
WEB http://www.intbc.com/sleuth/usen.html

> "PHOAKS: The acronym stands for 'people helping one another know stuff.' So cute."

➤ **PHOAKS** Tracks URLs mentioned in a few thousand Usenet groups. The acronym stands for "people helping one another know stuff." So cute. Search by a specific newsgroup name or browse the index by Usenet hierarchy (alt, comp, misc, rec, sci, soc, or talk). Results list the name of the Web page, who recommended the site, and when. You can also sort the resources by popularity and view a listing of other relevant sites.
WEB http://www.phoaks.com/phoaks/index.html

➤ **Search Dejanews** Dejanews archives posts from more than 13,000 newsgroups since March 1995 (although staff are working on archiving posts since 1979). This pow-

Location: http://www.dejanews.com/

The Premier Usenet Search Utility

Power Search!   Contacts   Bookmark DejaNews   Help Index

Quick Search For: [＿＿＿＿＿＿＿] [Find]

We've Got More Than Anybody Else — FIND OUT WHY — CLICK HERE

Click on graphic to visit site!

Copyright © 1996 Deja News Research Service, Inc. All rights reserved.

Dejanews is working on its long-term memory
http://www.dejanews.com

erful search utility enables you to search
Usenet messages by any keyword or text
fragment, including author's name, newsgroup, date, or subject. Filter queries by
newsgroup, date, or author. Search options enable you to tailor your results: retrieve an entire thread, sort messages by
relevance, newsgroup, date, or author;
match all or any keywords; limit the hits
per screen; or list oldest or newest
matches first. Clicking on the link to an
author's email address will produce an author's profile which lists the number of articles he or she posted and over what time
period, the percentage of articles which
were followups to other Usenet articles,
and a numerical breakdown of postings to
individual newsgroups.
WEB http://www.dejanews.com

SIFT (Stanford Information Filtering Tool)
Now in partnership with Reference.com,
SIFT offers advanced Usenet searching
capabilities with access to more than
16,000 newsgroups and 1,000 mailing lists
archived for the past month. Search by
subject, author, organization, conversa-

READ YOU SEE ME?

"Can the passive
reading (not post-
ing) and saving of
articles in the
'alt.conspiracy
.geraldo.rivera
.killed.ron.brown'
be tracked back to
the reader?"

"Saving would show
up in client back-
ups. Reading would
show up in news
server logs. Re-
trieving web pages
is logged by
client IP# against
each page, and
many server logs
are publicly ac-
cessible. For the
publicly accessi-
ble logs, it would
be straightforward
to search for all
IP#'s belonging
toa particular
company. I've even
seen server logs
show up in Alta
Vista searches.
(something_or
_other.uark.edu)"

—from **comp
.security.misc**

tional thread, newsgroup, mailing list, or keywords. Set search parameters such as month, day, and year; brief or full output format; and number of hits. Sort results by date, relevance, subject, name, login, host, organization, and groups. Registered users can also store their favorite search requests and re-run them automatically to return only new results since the last search.

WEB http://www.reference.com

EMAIL-GATE

"Make sure that your staff understands email is not secure. First, let your people know that email is not private. Email is often copied and reposted, much to the sender's dismay. As Carol Welsh of the Computer Museum says, "Don't say anything in email that you wouldn't want to read on the front page of the New York Times". Ask Tonya Harding. She made front page news during the 1994 Winter Olympics when reporters snooped in her email. Your employees may not have reporters poking in their mailboxes, but email industrial espionage is on the rise. Maybe your competitors snoop. Let your

How can I find out where someone has been surfing online?

Let's say it isn't up to the government what children are and are not allowed to see, and that it is the business of the parent how a child's mind is formed. A radical notion, perhaps, but one that by default is becoming the norm. Given the volume and kinds of information accessible through a telephone line, it is understandable that parents might want to keep watch on what their kids are download-

CyberSentry, traffic cop on the Information Superhighway
http://www.microsys.com/cybers

Location: http://www.microsys.com/cybers/

Welcome to The Cyber Sentry Briefing Room!

The Internet offers tremendous resources and opportunities to business. However, corporations are aware that these opportunities can potentially distract employees, affect productivity and endanger the integrity of the network. Cyber Sentry preserves productivity and maintains integrity for organizations that utilize the Internet as a key resource for their mission critical business.

Evaluate Cyber Sentry free for 30 days before you buy!

ing. Fortunately, there are a lot of new software programs that give parents the control they want.

In the business world, computer monitoring is also perfectly legal, and the software applications used are known as "productivity management tools." While no law requires that employers inform employees about their intention to monitor them electronically, it may be a good idea to do so. Only about 36 percent of companies with email have policies on its proper use in the workplace, but with increased public concern over privacy issues, employers might save themselves legal entanglements by clearly stating a formal policy. Parents can just lay some ground rules and let NetNanny do the rest.

➤ **Email Company Policy Considerations** Vince Emery's tips from February 3-5, archived at WebSuccess's Tips of the Day, cover topics related to company email policies.
WEB http://www.wgi.com/ar-feb96.html

➤ **Phone and Email Policy** Many employees may be under the impression that their phone and email communications are private. To eliminate confusion, employers may want to draw up an official phone and email policy. Here is a sample policy statement from a workshop conducted by Court TV's Small Business Law Center. Includes a sample employee acknowledgement form.
WEB http://www.courttv.com/seminars/handbook /fonemail.html

➤ **Technological Surveillance in the Workplace** The ethics and legalities of "monitoring

workers know that email may be used as legal evidence. The most famous example was during the Iran-Contra hearings, when Oliver North thought he had deleted his email. Actually, a backup system had saved his messages, which were used as evidence against him. Email was also used as evidence when Microsoft Corp. was investigated by the federal government. U.S. Justice Department investigators sifted through thousands of email messages from Microsoft employees, dating back years. And email has shown up in court as evidence in divorce cases."

—from **Email Company Policy Considerations**

I spy a fish
http://www.odd.net/ozarks/lakecam

email, computer files, voice mail, and telephone use without crossing the privacy line."

WEB http://www.fwlaw.com/techsurv.html

Software for spying on your minions

➤ **CyberSentry** Microsystems Software's corporate Internet access management tool.

- Monitors employee use of the Internet. Inhibits unauthorized activity and controls downloading of software to the network environment.
- Works with Windows, WIN 95, Microsoft Network.
- Costs about $50 per employee (less for volume purchases).

  WEB http://www.microsys.com/cybers

➤ **Internet WatchDog** Records all computer activity the way a telephone bill lists all the phone numbers called.

- Monitors all system functions. Keeps graphics logs and provides screen-shots of any computer activity at predetermined intervals.
- Works with PC (Windows 3.1 or Windows 95) or MAC (System 7.0 or higher).
- Costs $29.95.

  WEB http://www.algorithm.com/internet
  /watchdog.html

➤ **Mr. Burns** The "perfect Windows monitoring, metering, tracking, spying, and security product."

- Monitors which applications have been run, how often, and for how long; the number of keystrokes entered by the user; and system idle time. Runs undetected and maintains a daily log of us-

Location: http://www.webster.com/

WebTrack™: Internet Control and Monitoring Software

Answering the Enterprise need to forestall legal exposure from unwanted World Wide Web and Internet content; Providing the means to ensure overall enterprise productivity is enhanced by the Internet, not reduced by non-business related "surfing"; Providing reporting and analysis tools to measure, manage and improve enterprise Internet use.

Secure Computing Acquires Webster Network Strategies

How much Web can WebTrack track?
http://www.webster.com

age statistics.
* Works with any PC that supports MS Windows 3.x (networked or stand-alone). Download the shareware from the WINSHAR forum on CompuServe.
* Free (Shareware).

   WEB http://ourworld.compuserve.com/homepages /esmsoftware/mrburns.htm

Sequel Net Access Manager A server-based application that "lets you review your Internet usage with the same ease that you currently review your monthly telephone reports."
* Monitors all inbound/outbound traffic, including time of transaction, IP source address, destination, port number, packet size, and usage violations. Individual and group usage can be monitored by time, volume, activity or service type. A filtering engine enables control over access to Web servers, file transfering, newsgroups, email, Telnet, and commercial services like AOL.
* Works with Windows NT, Novell NetWare, OS/2, and most UNIX servers.
* Costs $89 per user (less for bulk licens-

ing). Downloadable demo is available at this site.

WEB http://www.sequeltech.com/product/snam

➤ **Snag: Secure Net Access Guardian** A server-based program that monitors, records, and controls Internet access for each workstation on a local network.

- Monitors all Internet acitivity, including sites accessed, with custom reporting capabilities.
- Works with Windows NT PC and manages all types of workstations including Macintosh, Windows, WIN 95, Windows NT, and Unix.
- Costs: For pricing details call (412) 531-5223.

WEB http://www.snag.com

➤ **TCPSpy** DN Software's "popular shareware TCP/IP network administration tool for DOS."

- Monitors data being sent along a TCP

One wrong cyberstep and NetNanny will pull the plug
http://www.netnanny.com

connection that has at least one partici-
pant on your local network.
* Works with MS-DOS.
* Costs $15 (shareware).
   WEB http://www.cs.orst.edu/~noord/dnsoftware

➤ **WebTrack** Because every step in cyberspace leaves a footprint.
   * Monitors all WebTrack-controlled URL
   accesses, both accepted and denied, including the date and time; also reports
   on corporate Internet usage (most active users, categories of sites visited,
   types of files accessed). Features "fine-
   sieve" filtering via a WebTrack Control
   List that you can edit.
   * Works with platforms AIX 3.2 & 4.1,
   BSD/OS, HP-UX, Linux, Silicon
   Graphics Irix 5.3, Solaris 2.4, SunOS
   4.1.3.
   * Costs: Call WNS Sales at 1-800-WNS-
   0066 for pricing information.
   WEB http://www.webster.com

Software for spying on your kids
➤ **Cyber Patrol**
   * Monitors, filters, and blocks all Internet
   access. Requires the CyberNOT Block
   List of access-denied URLs, which is
   updated regularly. The ChatGuard
   feature controls chatroom access.
   * Works with Macintosh or Windows.
   * Costs $29.95 for registered software
   plus a three-month subscription to the
   CyberNOT list (subsequent subscrip-
   tions cost $29.95 a year). Free demos of
   Cyber Patrol 3.0 and 2.11 are down-
   loadable at this site.
   WEB http://www.cyberpatrol.com

KEEPING TRACK OF SURFERS

hit: any connection to an Internet site, including inline image requests and errors

request: a hit that successfully retrieves content

visit: a series of consecutive requests from a user to an Internet site

user: anyone who visits the site at least once

organization: a commercial, academic, non-profit, government, or military entity that connects users to the Internet, identified by an entity's Internet domains

request duration: the time between two consecutive requests within the same visit

visit duration: the time between the first and last request of a visit

bandwidth: the number of bytes used in transmitting your content

geography: the continent, country, region, state, city, and ZIP code are based on an organization's Internet domain registration

> **CYBERsitter**
>   • Monitors all Internet activity, including attempts to access blocked material. Filters "bad sites" and phrases.
>   • Works with Windows 95 or Windows 3.1x.
>   • Costs $39.95. A free trial version is downloadable from this site.
>   WEB http://www.solidoak.com/cybersit.htm

"Total parental control. Violations trigger a shutdown of either the application or the computer."

> **Net Nanny** Total parental control. This software lets you monitor the kids' computer use and define what you want them to be able to access. Violations trigger a shutdown of either the application or the computer.
>   • Monitors all Internet and PC activity online or off, including TCP/IP streams, Web browsers, newsgroups, FTPs, IRC, email, and BBSs, as well as all offline Windows or DOS applications. Features full Internet filtering capability and controlled access to local PC files, drives, loading of unauthorized diskettes and CD-ROMS, and menu commands.
>   • Works with PC running MS-DOS v3.3, Windows v3.1, or Windows 95.
>   • Costs $39.95. A free evaluation copy is available at this site.
>   WEB http://www.netnanny.com

> **Tattle-Tale** Just monitor the kids' Internet use or restrict access at a level you control.

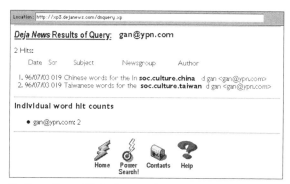

The Usenet history of NetSpy's senior editor
http://www.dejanews.com

* Monitors all Internet activity including sites visited and information exchanged. Reports include quicklinks to the sites visited so parents can verify their content.
* Works with Windows 3.1 or later, Windows 95, or Windows NT.
* Costs $29.95.
  WEB http://www.pond.com/~pearlsft

Software for tracking your Web site visitors

➤ **Bolero**
* Monitors the number of hits to your Web site, the time of day a user hits a page, and which sites are providing links to your Web site. A variety of reports can be generated, such as use by period, use over time, pages downloaded, bytes transferred, estimates of visit length, number of links accessed per visit, lists of popular entry and exit points, breakdown of use for specific domains and sub-domains, popularity of documents, summary information by domain, session and URL attributes, and errors. Bolero will be available in Bronze, Silver, and Gold editions for

increasing levels of functionality.

• Works with Windows NT, Unix, and Macintosh.

• Cost: Email info@everyware.com or call toll-free 1-888-819-2500 for prices.

WEB http://www.everyware.com/Bolero

➤ **CommunitySTATS** Tracks the "psychographics" of online visitors to your Web site. CommunitySTATS is part of Amicus's Community Builder set of applications, which also includes interactivity, security, database, and publishing software.

• Monitors the number of times a screen was accessed during a certain period, and the identity of participants who access the screen. Features custom reports at the group or individual level.

• Works with SQL database-capable platforms.

• Costs: Email info@amicaus.com for pricing details.

WEB http://www.amicus.com/tracking.htm

➤ **Intersé market focus 2**

• Monitors who visits your site (by individual and by organization) and from where (by continent, country, region, state, city, and even ZIP code), when, how long they stay, what kind of info they retrieve, and how many bytes they use to get it. Intersé also has its own newsgroup (interse.talk) and mailing list (subscription form at http://www.interse.com/infoexch).

• Works with all Web server software that supports the common log file format; Intersé market focus works with Windows NT and Windows 95.

- Costs $695 per Web site for a standard edition license.

WEB http://www.interse.com

▶ **Open Market Web Reporter 2.0** Web tracking with a Web browser-based and platform-independent graphical user interface.

- Monitors who visits your site, which links they follow and exactly where in your site they go, which site they came from and which site they go to next. It also features various customizable reporting options.
- Works with common log and extended log file formats; HTML, HTML 3.0, plain text (ASCII), and comma-separated plain text output formats.
- Costs $495 for the first CPU and $195 for each additional.

WEB http://www.openmarket.com/reporter

▶ **SiteTrack**

- Monitors who visits your site, which links they follow and exactly where in your site they go, which site they came

Intersé is focused on monitoring Web sites
http://www.interse.com

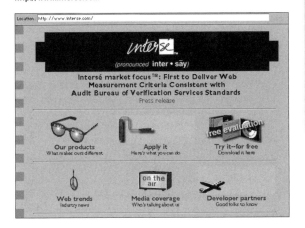

WHO'S BEHIND THAT DOMAIN?

Enter a domain name into any of the search engines below and find out the name of its owner, its real-life address, contact info for the system administrator, and a full history of the domain's previous names.

- **Gopher Whois Search**
  URL gopher://rs.internic .net/7waissrc%3A/rs /whois.src

- **IntelliNet Whois Query Service**
  WEB http://www.intellinet .com/CoolTools/Whois

- **NamesNet Domain Name Search**
  WEB http://www.names net.co.uk/search.html

- **Net Names International Internet Domain Name Registry**
  WEB http://www.net names.com

- **Web-Based Whois Search**
  WEB http://rs.internic .net/cgi-bin/itts/whois

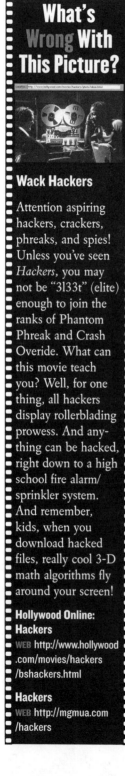

What's Wrong With This Picture?

Wack Hackers

Attention aspiring hackers, crackers, phreaks, and spies! Unless you've seen *Hackers*, you may not be "3l33t" (elite) enough to join the ranks of Phantom Phreak and Crash Overide. What can this movie teach you? Well, for one thing, all hackers display rollerblading prowess. And anything can be hacked, right down to a high school fire alarm/sprinkler system. And remember, kids, when you download hacked files, really cool 3-D math algorithms fly around your screen!

Hollywood Online: Hackers
WEB http://www.hollywood.com/movies/hackers/bshackers.html

Hackers
WEB http://mgmua.com/hackers

Speed-dialing was not an official sport of the 1996 Summer Olympics
http://www.olympic.att.com/village/govcamera/camera2.html

from and which site they go to next. A drop-in tool for tracking Web surfers' visits, it features on-the-fly interactivity allowing your Web site to adapt to the user in real-time.

- Works with a Netscape server that supports the Netscape Server API for shared libraries.
- Costs $3,495 per cpu license.
WEB http://www.cortex.net/sitetrack

Webthreads

- Monitors the activity of every Web site visitor, including what links they follow and how much time they spend at the site. Features an interactive extension using "iHTML," which allows content changes based on visitor input.
- Works with Linux, Linus/ELF, Sun Sparc Solaris 2.4/2.5. A free demo and the alpha version are downloadable from this site.
- Costs: For pricing info, email info@webthreads.com, or call 1-888-THREDIT.
WEB http://www.webthreads.com

spies "Я" us

Where are the real spies online?

I. **I want to find the online equivalent of Langley or MI5. Where are the real spies?**

If you knew where they were, how good could they be? Where to look at, listen to, and learn from the best in the business.

II. **I need to hire a private eye. How can I find one online?**

Find your own secret agent man to help you make your mission possible.

Where are the real spies online?

From Harry Lime in *The Third Man* to Harry Tasker in *True Lies*, the spies of fiction have long captured our imagination. But where and who are the real spies? Chances are they are lurking right under your nose, and if you knew who they were... Still, sometimes even the finest intelligence agent needs to hawk for business. So whether you need a professional spy on your side or you just want to see what those private eyes like to talk about, there are a few spy groups that make their presence known online. But remember, you can only see what they want you to see. The rest is strictly confidential.

I want to find the online equivalent of Langley or MI5. Where are the real spies?

One thing's for sure, they're not living at 12 Rue Madeleine. You can find real spies on the Net and it won't take you more than 39 steps to get to them. Don't be surprised if you run into some with golden eyes, fingers, or guns. Some even have a license to kill. Get online and get in like Flint.

General Intelligence
► **Intelligence and Counterintelligence** Three pages of links to sites on military, political, and non-military intelligence matters. Whether you're interested in the historical (Sun Tzu: *The Use of Spies*) or the practical (Sniper Country), this page will hook you right up to a source.
WEB http://www.kinsoft.com/kim-spy.htm

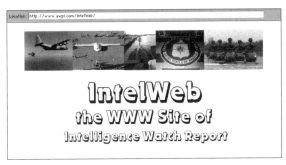

What they're up to, where, and for whom
http://awpi.com/IntelWeb

➤ **IntelWeb** Home of the Intelligence Watch Report, the only open source of daily updates on the world of global intelligence. Subscriptions to the email, fax, or hardcopy service run upwards of $100 a year. There are a few free tidbits at this Web site, including a bibliography, links to intelligence-related 'zines, and a list of acronyms. If you happen to require the services of a "professional," check out the resumés of trained analysts, cryptographers, investigators, and operational specialists in the IWR classifieds.
WEB http://awpi.com/IntelWeb

> **"You can find real spies on the Net and it won't take you more than 39 steps to get to them."**

➤ **P.I. Mall** A suburban oasis for private investigators in cyberspace. If you're a budding private eye (or just looking for one), this Web site should be your first stop. Shop for software, browse *P.I. Magazine*, link to invaluable online resources, or solve a murder just for fun by playing P.I. Mall's multimedia game, *Who Did It?*
WEB http://www.pimall.com

CIA FAQ

"What is so distinctive about the Central Intelligence Agency?"

"The CIA is purely a foreign intelligence organization and has no domestic security or law enforcement duties. The Agency's activities are governed by various statutes and Executive Orders and are overseen by Congressional Committees and executive bodies."

"How many people work for the Central Intelligence Agency and what is its budget?"

"Neither the number of employees nor the size of the Agency's budget can at present be publicly disclosed. A common misconception is that the Agency has an unlimited budget, which is far from true. While classified, the budget and size of the CIA are known in detail and scrutinized daily by the Office of Management and Budget and by the Intelligence Oversight and Defense Subcommittees of the Appropriations Committees in both houses of Congress.

▷ **The Secret Agent's Home Page** "Everything you always wanted to know about espionage, but were too afraid of the FBI to ask." Visit great spies in history at the Gallery of Espionage, practice your cryptography skills in the Decoding Room, read spy stories at the Spy's Bookshelf, and test your potential in the field with the Spy Quiz.
WEB http://www.aladdin.co.uk/dryden/spies/spies.htm

▷ **Spooks@WEB** Fun places to browse the world of spies, spooks, conspirators, and cryptographers.
WEB http://www.deltanet.com/users/llambert /shadow.html

▷ **The Spy Page** An index of fun and informative spy links from the James Bond Home Page to the Spy Shop.
WEB http://www.charweb.org/government/spy.html

▷ **Virtual World of Spies and Intelligence** Links to mostly just-for-fun Web sites on everything from covert news to counter-terrorism.
WEB http://www.dreamscape.com/frankvad/covert.html

Watching the Detectives

▷ **alt.private.investigator** Sherron writes: "I have the name, SSN, current address, DOB, and car tag number of a subject. Is there a database I can use to track where he moves to next? Or do I have to do it the old fashioned way?" Amid the spy book teasers and private investigators advertising their services, everyday netsurfers can post requests for inside info and hope the sleuths speak up.
USENET alt.private.investigator

➤ **Private Eye Mailing List** If you want to be a private investigator (or just look like one), subscribe to this mailing list and become privy to a world of tips, tricks, pitfalls, and professional topics. Subscriptions are not automatic for this list, but if you're approved, you can discuss such covert operations as accident reconstruction software and the legal conditions for interstate wiretapping.

EMAIL listproc@list.intnet.net ✍ *Type in message body:* subscribe private eye ⟨Your Name⟩

G-Men

➤ **CIA** Unless you're a hacker, you're probably not going to find any top secrets here, but you can go on a virtual tour of CIA headquarters (something you can't do in real life) and view a video clip of President Truman signing the National Security Act which mandated the creation of the agency in 1947. You can also skim through seven CIA publications, includ-

---

Take the virtual tour of Langley
http://www.odci.gov/cia

Location: http://www.odci.gov/cia/information/tour/lobbyseal.html

Original Headquarters Building Lobby - CIA Seal

In the main lobby of the Original Headquarters Building, a large granite CIA seal is laid on the lobby floor. The radiating spokes of the compass rose depict the coverage of intelligence data from all areas of the world to a central point.

"Does the CIA spy on Americans? Does it keep a file on me?"

"The Central Intelligence Agency is expressly prohibited by Executive Order from routinely engaging in the domestic use of such techniques as electronic, mail, or physical surveillance; monitoring devices; or unconsented physical search. Such intrusion into the lives of Americans by any Government agency could take place only under the most extraordinary conditions of concern for the national welfare and, even then, only when approved by the Attorney General. CIA does not maintain files on American citizens. Names of U.S. citizens may appear in various records as a consequence of routine business they conduct with the CIA, but they are in no way segregated for surveillance or special attention. Any citizen has the right to confirm this fact under the authority of the Privacy Act."

—from **CIA**

ABBREVS. & ACRONYMS

"**ACOUSTINT** Acoustic Intelligence

COMINT Communications Intelligence

COMSEC Communications Security

ELINT Electronic Intelligence

FISINT Foreign Instrumentation Signals Intelligence

HUMINT Human Intelligence

IMINT Imagery Intelligence

INFOSEC Information Security

LASINT Laser Intelligence

MASINT Measurement and Signature Intelligence

OSCINT Open Sources Intelligence

RADINT Radar Intelligence

SIGINT Signals Intelligence

SIGSEC Signals Security

TAREX Target Exploitation

TELINT Telemetry Intelligence"

—from **IntelWeb**

ing its *Handbook of International Economic Statistics* and the *1995 Factbook on Intelligence*. But don't get too excited—the *Factbook* links mostly to historical documents about CIA history and job descriptions of its director and deputy director positions.
WEB http://www.odci.gov/cia

Federal Bureau of Investigation Can the Feds be "called in" to investigate a serious crime when local police cannot solve the case? How can I get an FBI security clearance? How does the FBI select its "Ten Most Wanted Fugitives?" Find the answers to these frequently asked questions at the bureau's home page. Then, peruse the lineup of wanted criminals and current FBI investigations. Rewards are offered if you can help solve a case.
WEB http://www.fbi.gov

US Secret Service They're not just bodyguards for the president, former presi-

Another one bites the dust
http://www.fbi.gov

Location: http://www.fbi.gov/rickalb.htm

WANTED BY THE FBI
Rickey Allen Bright
Unlawful Flight to Avoid Prosecution - Kidnapping, Rape, and Sexual Assault of a Minor

CAPTURED

Rickey Allen Bright

CONSIDERED ARMED AND DANGEROUS WITH SUICIDAL TENDENCIES. TAKE NO ACTION TO APPREHEND THIS PERSON YOURSELF. REPORT ANY INFORMATION TO THE NEAREST FBI FIELD OFFICE.

dents, and their families. The Secret Service allegedly set up an undercover BBS to catch cell phone and Unix hackers. This official government page contains a full list of agents' duties which include investigating criminal violations pertaining to computer fraud, credit card fraud, and U.S. securities.

WEB http://www.ustreas.gov/treasury/bureaus/usss /usss.html

Investigative Associations

➤ **Association of Independent Information Professionals** Commercial information brokers constitute the membership of the AIIP. Its members are experts in online database searching, market and industry surverys, public records research, competitive intelligence, and document delivery.

WEB http://www.intNet.net/aiip

➤ **Institute of Advanced Investigative Studies** Have you dreamed of becoming a certified investigator of fraud or computer crime? Well, wake up! This institute will provide wou with training, education, and certification.

WEB http://www.pimall.com/iais/iais.html

➤ **Investigative Reporters and Editors** Investigative reporters never reveal their sources. They have a lot in common with detectives and spies, except that journalists make their findings available to the public. Live vicariously through the *IRE Journal* and the IRE-L mailing list (details at this site). Find out why whistleblowing takes a lot more than just putting your lips together.

WEB http://www.ire.org

What's Wrong With This Picture?

Why We Can Make Plans For August

1. Apple computers, however incompatible they are with other earthly systems, *are* compatible with computers on alien spacecraft.

2. Powerbooks are so compatible that no direct connection is needed for file transfer.

3. So compatible, in fact, that the mere command "upload virus" is enough to eradicate an otherwise omnipotent species.

4. And alien technology has not progressed to the point of a virus scan.

Independence Day
WEB http://www.cyber beach.net/~rchartra /id4.htm

WEB http://www.holly wood.com/movies /independ/photo

Your eyes will witness results with these investigators
http://www.eyewitness.com

➤ **Investigator's Open Network** Dedicated to proper use of information technology to enhance the investigation industry, ION members benefit from training opportunities, a newsletter, and special insurance rates. ION provides a screening and referral service for those in need of private investigative services. Its database contains more than 23,000 investigators.
WEB http://www.pihome.com/ioninc

➤ **National Association of Investigative Specialists, Inc.** A trade association of private investigative professionals. Its home page contains information about NAIS seminars, workshops, books, and publications, as well as hotlinks to investigative resources online.
WEB http://www.pimall.com/nais/home.html

➤ **National Institute for Computer-Assisted Reporting** Offers education, training, and events in the use of computer analysis and research for journalists. At this Web site, find out how to access the NICAR mailing list and newsgroups and how to get your carpal tunnel hands on *Computer-Assisted Reporting: A Practical Guide*.
WEB http://www.nicar.org

I need to hire a private eye. How can I find one online?

Uncomfortable with a cloak and dagger? Still can't seem to get smart? There are plenty of men with one red shoe who will see you through your clear and present danger... For a list, see "Full-service P.I.s," Appendix III, p. 171.

COUNTERSPY

privacy

I. Why should I be concerned about my privacy on the Internet?

Prying eyes could be watching you. Here's how they're doing it, and what you can do about it.

II. Who's looking after my cyber-rights?

These groups care about your privacy so much, they're willing to fight for it online and in court.

I know I can run, but can I hide?

At www.careers.org, you can search for the high-paid position of your dreams, without leaving your office cubicle. You can email your resumé to dozens of prospective employers, and even receive a real-time job counseling session in a chat room. Does this mean that you should feel free to explore your options from the comfort of your company-issue swivel chair? Probably not, unless you feel like searching for a new job from the unemployment line.

> "Think of the Internet as a field of freshly fallen snow. Every time you surf the Net, you leave a unique set of footprints."

While this may sound like a case of paranoia, if you're using your company-provided Internet access, it is not only possible, but also increasingly probable that you are being monitored. Think of the Internet as a field of freshly fallen snow. Every time you surf the Net, send an email message, or post to a newsgroup, you leave a unique set of footprints, which may be tracked by anyone with even the slightest expertise in this area.

Why should I be concerned about my privacy on the Internet?

According to a recent survey conducted by the Society for Human Resources Management, "36 percent of organizations

See what's cookin' in the Berkeley Systems Kitchen
http://www.berksys.com/www/funtour/takepic.html

that provide email look at their employees' email records for business necessity or security; 8 percent conduct random reviews of the email. A whopping 75 percent responded that employers should have the right to read company-provided email." This last figure is up 14 percent from a 1993 survey.

Policy to protect your rights is akin to putting a plastic do-not-disturb sign on the Ho Jo's door knob. Technology long ago outpaced policy. Is the postman allowed to drool over your romantic postcards? Of course not. Can he do so? Absolutely, if he's voyeuristically inclined and willing to risk his job.

So while you're busy spying on others, you should be sure that you're not being spied on yourself. And the best way to protect your own privacy is by arming yourself against technology *with* technology. Start by reading about the issues, and then check out some of the general resources to begin trading in your do-not-disturb sign for a pack of rabid German shepherds.

WATCHING YOUR HIDE

"If you use a computer at work, it's probably connected to a lot of other systems on a network. Most of the software packages that keep networks up and running have other features that allow system administrators to monitor things like how many pages you've printed, what files you've copied, when you logged in, and so on. Some programs, such as Novell's NetWare, even let administrators remotely access files on your computer desktop--without your knowing about it.... Most network management programs can be set up to keep a copy of every message sent or received within a company. Who's going to read through all that mail, you ask? That's where the computer comes in handy. Sophisticated search capabilities make it easy to glean certain keywords, like sex or resume. Even if your

Bosses with X-Ray Eyes Biased fodder for paranoids, this stringent critique of workplace monitoring nevertheless contains many an entertaining anecdote. Poor Gayle suffered a nervous breakdown under the strain of her boss' electronic omniscience. The article also lists some of the reason for the transcendence of Big Brother into the realm of the real. The monitoring of productivity is the most commonly cited justification. Some employers fear for their security, while still others simply want to ensure that their employees don't surf the Net on company time.

WEB http://www.macworld.com/password/mwlinks/xray.html

Privacy in the Digital Age A recent *c/net* article offers an excellent overview of the privacy issue, with particular emphasis on the individual in the workplace. The article dispels any self-righteous misconceptions workers might have about their rights, citing court cases that have set the precedent for the legality of workplace

Don't look now, but your privacy is being compromised
http://www.cnet.com/Content/Features/Dlife/Privacy

Location: http://www.cnet.com/Content/Features/Dlife/Privacy/

privacy in the digital age

special report:

part 1: who's watching you online?

by Susan Stellin

If you're reading this article at work, it's a safe bet that you're no stranger to company-provided Internet access--and chances are your boss also provides you with monitoring. Your boss can keep a copy of every email you send (*Flanagan et al. vs. Epson America, Inc.*), lest you disclose company secrets (*Borland vs. Wang, Eubanks, and Symantec*), or curse your superiors (*Michael A. Smyth vs. Pillsbury Company*). Be sure to check out the section of letters from readers who have experienced workplace monitoring firsthand.

WEB http://www.cnet.com/Content/Features/Dlife/Privacy

➤ **Workplace Monitoring** This 1993 fact sheet from the concerned citizens of the Privacy Rights Clearinghouse addresses all aspects of workplace privacy, from telephone to computer monitoring.

WEB http://www.acusd.edu/~prc/fs/fs7-work.html

I'm really worried now. Where can I read more?

➤ **alt.privacy** This heavily trafficked newsgroup is an excellent place to go for the latest buzz on privacy issues and technology. The regulars are a pretty homogenous bunch of anti-establishment, hi-tech privacy junkies.

USENET alt.privacy

➤ **Anonymity and Privacy on the Internet** One of the most cogent and comprehensive resources on the issue, including an excellent set of links to remailing and encryption resources, as well as FAQs.

WEB http://www.stack.urc.tue.nl/~galactus/remailers

➤ **comp.society.privacy** Discuss the issues with other concerned computer users.

USENET comp.society.privacy

network doesn't automatically keep copies of email, it's probably programmed to make backups. When you read your email, a copy is downloaded to your hard drive, so when the network gets backed up, your mail gets copied, too.

Software programs like Net Access Manager, WebTrack, and Internet WatchDog enable employers to secretly monitor what their employees are doing online—including the Web sites they visit, the amount of time spent there, and what types of files they download. A sample WebTrack report, for instance, details activity in categories such as "alternative journal," "entertainment," "job search," "sex," and "worthless." Besides snooping on employees, some of these programs allow employers to block certain online activity or to limit access time."

—from **Privacy in the Digital Age**

➤ **Ethical Issues in Electronic Information Systems** Excellent set of information related to privacy, network access, workplace monitoring, junk mailing, and general ethics. Useful facts and information are included along with the philosophizing.
URL ftp://ftp.cc.utexas.edu/pub/grg/gcraft/notes/ethics/ethics.html

➤ **Ethics** Links to mailing lists, publications, and papers on the ethics of privacy in cyberspace.
WEB http://www.cs.unca.edu/~davidson/ethics.html

➤ **HotWired and Wired Privacy Archive** A set of articles and resources from the publications that made it cool to be a geek.
WEB http://www.hotwired.com/clipper/index.html

➤ **Privacy Forum Archive** Check out past issues of the publication devoted to the discussion of online privacy issues.
WEB http://www.vortex.com/privarch.htm

➤ **Privacy Links** Includes organizations, mailing lists, software, and related home pages.
WEB http://wwwl.netaxs.com:8080/people/bmc/privacy.html

➤ **Privacy Resources** Excellent resource with a few links to non-English sites.
WEB http://newciv.org/worldtrans/sov/privacy.html

➤ **Privacy Resources FAQ** Where to go, online and off, to safeguard your privacy.
WEB http://www.scn.org/fp/admin/cpsr/Privacy-guide.txt

When it comes to protecting your privacy, the **ACLU** has a clue
http://www.aclu.org

➤ **Security and Encryption Links** An astound-
ingly thorough and varied set of links to
everything from cypherpunk and cryp-
torebel resources to interception and monitoring tools.
WEB http://www.cs.auckland.ac.nz/~pgut001/links.html

➤ **Security vs. Access** A collection of articles
on security and privacy from 1992 to 1995.
WEB http://www-lib.usc.edu/~dhwong/mar5.html

Who's looking after my cyber-rights?

The recent anti-censorship victory in the
ACLU vs. Reno defeated the Communications Decency Act and its attempt to instill
family values online. Furthermore, despite its
efforts to the contrary, the government has no
national control over privacy safeguards such
as encryption and remailers. These rights

break down, however, when the encryption debate enters the realm of national security and the encryption of messages over international boundaries. Battle lines are currently drawn around the export control policies. Adorning home pages, blue ribbons and golden keys symbolize commitment to anti-censorship and encryption rights, as advocacy groups inform the public from their home pages.

"The government has no national control over privacy safeguards like encryption and remailers."

> **A Declaration of Independence of Cyberspace** John Perry Barlow's attack against government intervention in cyberspace.
> WEB http://www.netfreedom.org.au/anoid/nfjpbdec.htm

> **ACLU** Read all about the ACLU's winning battle against the indecency provisions of the Communications Decency Act.
> WEB http://www.aclu.org

I spy trains for tots
http://www.uso.com/eic/tiny.html

Location: http://www.uso.com/eic/tiny.html

TINY TOWN, COLORADO
The Oldest Kid Sized Village and Railroad in USA

LIVE CAMERA PICTURE OF TRAIN STATION (WHEN RUNNING)

Andre Bacard's Home Page One of the world's leading experts on computer privacy alternately terrifies and informs with his contention that the Internet is not safe, and his FAQs on what to do about it. The site also links to Bacard's *Playboy* interview entitled, "The Computers Have Eyes."
WEB http://www.well.com/user/abacard

Center for Democracy and Technology A nonprofit organization dedicated to promoting constitutional civil liberties and democratic values in new computer and communications technologies. CDT's Privacy Issues and Demonstration Site features privacy resources and an interactive demo showing what its Web server can find out about you. The site also includes a chart of the privacy policies of the major online commercial services. Information includes whether or not the user can have more than one identity, whether the service monitors its chatrooms, and if the service retains a copy of email even after the user has downloaded it.
WEB http://www.cdt.org/index.html

Computer Professionals for Social Responsibility An alliance of computer professionals and others interested in the impact of computer technology on society. In 1994 its program office for privacy and civil liberties spun off to become the Electronic Privacy Information Center, but CPSR still posts information about the organization's privacy activities at its Web site.
WEB http://snyside.sunnyside.com/home

CASE CLOSED

"The Internet may fairly be regarded as a never-ending worldwide conversation. The Government may not, through the CDA, interrupt that conversation. As the most participatory form of mass speech yet developed, the Internet deserves the highest protection from governmental intrusion."
—Judge Stewart Dalzell, ACLU v. Reno

"Have you ever heard of the Ninth Amendment? If you haven't here it is: 'The enumeration in the Constitution, of certain rights, shall not be construed to deny or disparage others retained by the people.' The "right to privacy", though not enumerated (i.e. not mentioned) in the Constitution, does not mean it does not exist. The biggest challenge we face is the fact the Supreme Court Justices are interjecting personal bias, into their rulings and not Constitutional interpretation as is their job."

—from **Privacy mailing list**

▶ **The Electronic Frontier Foundation** A nonprofit civil liberties organization dedicated to protecting privacy, free expression, and access to online resources and information. The highly visible EFF has been actively involved in a landmark case challenging the federal government's restrictions on the export of cryptography software; it also maintains an archive of information about privacy, surveillance, and cryptography.
WEB http://www.eff.org

▶ **Electronic Privacy Information Center** EPIC is a public-interest research center established to protect privacy, the First Amendment, and "constitutional values." This may sound like a somewhat nebulous mission, but EPIC has demonstrated an unflagging commitment to online privacy. Its site maintains an extensive list of privacy resources, including organizations, publications, conferences, and newsgroups, as well as a privacy archive of online documents and articles.
WEB http://www.epic.org

▶ **The Golden Key Campaign** Proudly display a key and envelope on your home page to show support for the campaign to protect "the essential human right to privacy."
WEB http://www.eff.org/goldkey.html

▶ **Internet Privacy Coalition** With a mission to "promote privacy and security on the Internet through widespread public availability" of privacy resources, the Internet Privacy Coalition is also founder of the Golden Key Campaign, which encourages people to display a key on their Web

WHERE CAN I READ MORE ABOUT THE LAW?

- **ACLU vs. Reno**
WEB http://www.eff.org
/Alerts/HTML/960612
_acluv_reno_decision
.html

- **The Electronic Communication Privacy Act**
WEB http://www.eff.org
/pub/Legislation/ecpa.law

- **Is There a Court in Cyberspace?**
WEB http://www.commlaw
.com/pepper/Memos/Info
Law/internet.102094.html

- **Legal Overview: The Electronic Frontier and the Bill of Rights**
WEB http://www.eff.org
/pub/Legal/bill_of_rights
_online.paper

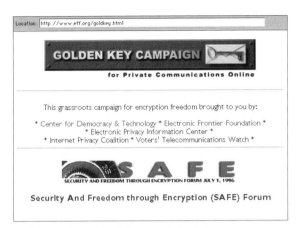

Location: http://www.eff.org/goldkey.html

GOLDEN KEY CAMPAIGN

for Private Communications Online

This grassroots campaign for encryption freedom brought to you by:

* Center for Democracy & Technology * Electronic Frontier Foundation *
* Electronic Privacy Information Center *
* Internet Privacy Coalition * Voters' Telecommunications Watch *

S A F E

SECURITY AND FREEDOM THROUGH ENCRYPTION FORUM JULY 1, 1996

Security And Freedom through Encryption (SAFE) Forum

The Golden Key Campaign unlocks the mysteries of private communications
http://www.eff.org/goldkey.html

pages in support of the right to privacy.
WEB http://www.privacy.org/ipc

➤ **Privacy International** Formed in 1990 as a watchdog on surveillance by governments and corporations. The emphasis here is on knowing and keeping up with the enemy, through articles such as "Big Brother Goes High Tech." Is DigiCash really anonymous? Privacy International doesn't think so, and concerned online customers can find out why.
WEB http://www.privacy.org/pi

> **"Is DigiCash really anonymous? Privacy International doesn't think so, and concerned online customers can find out why."**

➤ **The Privacy Rights Clearinghouse** PRC is a nonprofit consumer education and research program administered by the University of San Diego School of Law. PRC's somewhat outdated fact sheets offer practical, consumer-oriented informa-

Location: http://www.gomontana.com/presscam.html

Bozeman Daily Chronicle

Index

Extras Drawer

search

Welcome to Montana's first and only WebCam site.

1 Chronicle PressCam

Press Cam! *...Also check out our Skycam Weather page!*

Another day, another deadline at the *Bozeman Daily Chronicle*
http://www.gomontana.com/presscam.html

tion on topics ranging from cellular phone eavesdropping to employee monitoring. PRC also operates a telephone hotline that consumers can call for information about privacy issues.

WEB http://pwa.acusd.edu/~prc

▷ **Voters Telecommunications Watch** Free speech and the decriminalization of Crypto Exporting are the focus of this group's advocacy efforts. The site publishes BillWatch as well as FAQs on Internet parental control and the Communications Decency Act.

WEB http://www.vtw.org

anonymity

I. **I want to keep myself concealed. What's the easiest way to send email anonymously?**

Don't let the eyes have it: Put your email in a cyber-envelope.

II. **That's a start. But what if I want to be anonymous *and* private?**

Alpha.c2.org combines encryption and remailing for that extra layer of defense.

III. **Okay. I'm anonymous and I'm private. What will make me untraceable?**

Cypherpunk and mixmasters are so anonymous, you may not even recognize your own email.

IV. **And the Web? How can I visit sites invisibly?**

Covert surfing in six easy pieces.

How do I make myself disappear?

So your email aren't as safe as you thought they were. You've expressed lust for your co-workers, animosity towards your boss, and a chocolate fetish, all in the equivalent of an online postcard. It's too late to change the past, but you can safeguard future email against potential exposure.

Is the postcard analogy a fair one? Actually, yes. Like a postcard, an email message passes through network after network before finally reaching its destination. And even then, privacy is not assured. Some commercial services keep email on file after it's been downloaded. And as explained in the chapter on privacy, just as nothing stands between your erotic musings and the postman, save his own moral fiber, your email is at the mercy of system operators everywhere.

Of course, only an idiot (or an exhibitionist) pours out his innermost secrets on a postcard. What's an envelope for, after all, if not to keep out prying eyes. With a mixture of pragmatism and knowledge, you can put your email in a kind of cyberenvelope—one that is held together by stronger stuff than foul-tasting glue.

One way to keep people from knowing your business online is to send your mail anonymously. While someone might still be able to read it, they won't know the identity of the sender. In snail-mail terms, this is the equivalent of sending a postcard with no signature. Online, however, it's a lot more complicated.

REMAIL TERMS

pseudoanonymous remailer: Entails the opening of an account with a remail operator. In other words, the operators know your remail address, which might not be ideal if you believe the old adage, "A chain is only as strong as its weakest link." The main advantage of the pseudo-anonymous system is, of course, its ease, because someone does all the work for you.

anonymous remailer: Much harder to use than their pseudo-anonymous cousins, truly anonymous remailers are the real thing, and they come in two varieties: mixmaster and cypherpunk.

Your identifying "footprint" is not a result of your signature, but of the outgoing "mailbox" from which you send your message.

As an example, imagine top executive Cindy is having an affair and wants to meet her young and studly lover for an uninterrupted tryst in Acapulco. She tells her beloved yet hapless husband, Jack, that she has an important business conference in, say, Cleveland, and off she goes, assured of success. "Send me a postcard, honey!" are unsuspecting Jack's parting words as Cindy steps out the door, bikini-filled suitcase in hand.

What's a cheating spouse to do? Now, if Cindy only had a blank Cleveland postcard lying around the house, she could scrawl a few loving words, find someone on a Cleveland-bound flight and ask them to post it for her when they arrived. Hapless Jack would be none the wiser. This is the basic principle of anonymous remailers.

cypherpunk: Takes messages, strips them of all headers, and sends them to recipients. This can make it difficult, but not impossible (see "encrypted reply blocks") to receive a reply.

mixmaster: A complicated remail system designed to withstand monitoring from even the most technically adept attacker.

encrypted reply blocks: A system which allows the recipient to respond to your email without compromising the secrecy of your address.

chaining remailers: Sending email through more than one remailer for extra anonymity protection.

I want to keep myself concealed. What's the easiest way to send email anonymously?

An anonymous remailing system either gives you an anonymous email address to which other people can send you mail, which is then forwarded to your real address (this system is sometimes referred to as a pseudo-anonymous server), or it posts or mails your message without any trace of your address. As long as you're not dealing with classified secrets, pseudoanonymous remailers are the easiest way to keep yourself undercover.

Anonymous remailers are also well-suited for impulsive posting to newsgroups. For example, as a diversion from your online sleuthing you may be roaming alt.tv.friends and find you have an irresistible urge to comment on the thread concerning Courtney Cox's wages. But you certainly don't want your email address plastered in the newsgroup for other *Friends* freaks to see. An unaltered Usenet post contains a header, complete with your name and email address. And if you don't want to share your email address with the denizens of, say, alt.psychotics—or with companies that cull email addresses for electronic junkmailing purposes—you might want to consider posting with an anonymous remailer. Anon.penet.fi, although less secure than some others, works admirably as a poster to Usenet. One method allows you to crosspost to multiple newsgroups, while the other does not. In both cases, replies to your post will be sent to anon.penet.fi, who will then forward them to you. Thanks to remailers, you can flame without fear.

"If you don't want to share your email address with the denizens of alt.psychotics, you might want to post with an anonymous remailer."

▶ **anon.penet.fi Unofficial FAQ** With more than 50,000 users in its database, the anon.penet.fi anonymous forwarding service is the most popular anonymous server on the Internet. It assigns each user a unique ID, which is used to allow others to send you email anonymously. It also offers a mail-to-news posting service,

The next bus is at 4 p.m.
http://www.geocities.com/cgi-bin/main/BHI/camera2.html

so that you can also post Usenet messages anonymously. But depsite its widespread popularity, anon.penet.fi is, unfortunately, not particularly secure. As a pseudo-anonymous service, anon.penet.fi keeps a database with every user's ID and corre-sponding email address. However, it is possible to use the service in conjunction with PGP (see the chapter on encryp-tion). For more information on anon.penet.fi, visit this FAQ, or contact the service directly by sending email to help@anon.penet.fi. The contact of your message doesn't matter; the mail robot is instructed to automatically send a you help file.

WEB http://www.stack.urc.tue.nl/~galactus/remailers/penet.html#whatis

➤ **Anonymous Remailer Non-technical FAQ** An important first stop on any cybersleuth's foray into the anonymous and pseudo-anonymous world of email privacy, this cogent FAQ by Andre Bacard, author of the *Computer Privacy Handbook,* offers clear explanations and breaks down the options. Happily, the very first question is, "What is a remailer?" and Bacard proceeds accordingly, taking no previous knowledge for granted. The FAQ's only flaw is the infrequency of its updates, and is therefore not recommended if you're hoping to keep up with the very latest advances.

WEB http://www.well.com/user/abacard/remail.html

▶ **List of Anonymous Remailers** Raph Levien's comprehensive list of remailers, including their PGP (Pretty Good Privacy) public keys. Along with the list, Levien has included an options and features section to help users choose the optimum remailer for their purposes.

WEB http://www.cs.berkeley.edu/~raph/remailer-list .html

▶ **Penet and the MacIntosh** Help for those using Eudora to post to Usenet.

WEB http://www.stack.urc.tue.nl/~galactus/remailers /macintosh.html

▶ **penet.michigass** Read all about the raid on anon.penet.fi that resulted in the revelation of a user's real name and address. That's not enough to pique you interest? How about this: The scientologists play a starring roll in the fiasco.

WEB http://www.tezcat.com/~wednsday/penet .michigass

▶ **Penet Remailer Help** Instructions and contact information by the service's operator, Julf. Anon.penet.fi doesn't support encryption, which means that messages

IS THERE A WAY TO REMAIL FROM THE WEB?

Not the most secure method of remailing, but certainly the most convenient, remailing forms allow you to paste your mail into ready-made documents, select the remailer or remailers you want to use, and send at the touch of a button.

● **Community ConneXion Premail**
  WEB http://www.c2.net

● **Remailing Over the World Wide Web**
  WEB http://www.stack.urc .tue.nl/~galactus/remailers /index-www.html

Location: http://www.otec.com/park-cam.html

OTEC's view of Bryant Park

Behind the New York Public Library the garden is quiet... for now
http://www.otec.com/park-cam.html

can be read en route to penet. The system's following is dwindling, as it has been all but usurped by far more secure systems.

WEB http://www.cs.berkeley.edu/~raph/penet.html

That's a start. But, what if I want to be anonymous *and* private?

Sometimes being anonymous isn't enough. Sometimes you need to be anonymous and incomprehensible.

➤ **Alpha.c2.org** Alpha is a pseudoanonymous remailer similar to anon.penit.fi, but more secure because it supports encryption. The FAQ includes instructions
WEB http://www.stack.urc.tue.nl/~galactus/remailers /alpha.html

➤ **Alpha.c2.org FAQ** Includes instructions for building an encrypted reply block.
WEB http://www.well.com/user/abacard/alpha.html

WHY USE A REMAILER?

"Why would YOU use remailers?"

"Maybe you're a computer engineer who wants to express opinions about computer products, opinions that your employer might hold against you. Possibly you live in a community that is violently intolerant of your social, political, or religious views. Perhaps you're seeking employment via the Internet and you don't want to jeopardize your present job. Possibly you want to place personal ads.

"Perchance you're a whistle-blower afraid of retaliation. Conceivably you feel that, if you criticize your government, Big Brother will monitor you. Maybe you don't want people 'flaming' your corporate e-mail address. In short, there are many legitimate reasons why you, a law abiding person, might use remailers."

—from **Anonymous Remailer Non-technical FAQ**

➤ **PGP Public Keys of Remailers that Support Encryption** A list of remailers for those who want the extra privacy of encryption, courtesy of privacy expert Raph Levien.
WEB http://kiwi.cs.berkeley.edu/pgpkeys

Okay. I'm anonymous and I'm private. What will make me untraceable?

Offhand, it might be hard to envision a situation that would require more anonymity than that provided by a pseudoanonymous remailer. After all, what's the fun of posting provocative messages to your favorite newsgroup if you can't read the outraged replies? But companies have their email secrets, as do governments, intelligence agencies, and just about everyone else for that matter. So, for those who crave the the next level in anonymity, both the mixmaster and cypherpunk remailers go the distance, by stripping your mail of all headers before forwarding them to their intended recipient. Still, even though the two remailers perform the same function, there are experts who can trace cypherpunk remailings to their source. Mixmaster remailings, on the other hand, and at least for now, should be completely untraceable.

"What's the fun of posting provocative messages to your favorite newsgroup if you can't read the outraged replies?"

➤ **Chaining Remailers Help** Realize the ultimate in email secrecy with this concise how-to for the chaining of remailers.
WEB http://www.replay.com/staff/usura/chain.html

▶ **Creating Encrypted Reply Blocks** An encrypted reply block allows recipients to respond to your message without giving away your address. This site lists 12 easy steps for creating such a block. Step 1: Get a copy of Private Idaho.
WEB http://www.stack.urc.tue.nl/~galactus/remailers/reply-blocks.html

▶ **Cypherpunk Remailers** Learn all about cypherpunk remailers and your options when using them. Use chain remailers (which use more than one remailer) to email your top secret chocolate chip cookie recipe, or exploit the wonders of premail, a service which automatically chains messages for cypherpunks, selects reliable remailers, and then performs the PGP encryption process.
WEB http://www.stack.urc.tue.nl/~galactus/remailers/index-cpunk.html

▶ **The John Doe Home Page** A downloadable computer program that does all of the work for you, combining encryption and remailers to provide anonymity and privacy ("Anonymity: No one need know who you are. Privacy—Your System

Keep 'em guessing with the mortuary assistant's friend, John Doe
http://www.compulink.co.uk/~net-services/jd.htm

Location: http://www.compulink.co.uk/~net-services/jd.htm

The John Doe Home Page
(Skip straight to download section)

Do you worry about your privacy on the Internet? Then read on for some unique solutions. This low cost technology uses encryption with a special "remailer" and gives you these astounding features:

● Anonymity - no one need know who you are
● Privacy - Your System Admin *cannot* read your mail
● Double Privacy - Your System Admin doesn't know who you are talking to
● Security - A compromised remailer does *not* compromise you

GET DOWN WITH PGP

"Anonymous Remailer ‹hfinney @shell.portal.com›

"510-bit key, Key ID 5620D5, created 1992/11/15

"---BEGIN PGP PUBLIC KEY BLOCK-----

"Version: 2.3

"mQBNAisGf+IAAAEB/
ieS6th8hIlQBjGpmct
VvsIxZBtmpykVXc3ps
hOXVfH4sECSugouk2z
m/PJtt59A2E5SO3xjp
DjeKlkQ745WINUABRG
OLFJlbWFpbGluZyBTZ
XJ2aWNlIIDxoZmlubmV
5QHNoZWxsLnBvcnRhb
C5jb20+iQCVAgUQK3A
zm4OA7OpLWtYzAQHza
wQAwZPaJUR9iNwyKMD
m4bRSaoOuu38lpq6rR
3nwORI+DSLKTXPqDaT
3xBmLdVvlPVguLcoao
/TRLkAheV7CIxodEiI
91AC2o6lqSXCP+vm3j
YmulSgUlKafXYbjLAb
ZpsKRAUjCpyxOwlYmo
HhkA+NZDzMcWp6/l/r
M/Vli4Jbt2+GJAJUCB
RArBpKvqBMDrlghTDc
BAST1BACfTqODpVubl
5MK5A4i6eiqU8MDQGW
OPOwUovPkNjscH2210
AfRteXEUM+nB+Xwkl6
RG/GdrG8r9PbWzSCx6
nBYb7FjOnPnRPtS/u6
9THNTF2gU2BDOj2vZF
811EHOYy6===arSc"

"---END PGP PUBLIC KEY BLOCK---"

—from **PGP Public Keys of Remailers that Support Encryption**

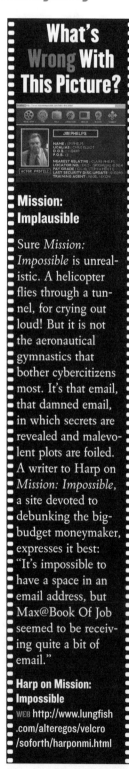

What's Wrong With This Picture?

JIM PHELPS

NAME: JIM PHELPS
U.CALIAS: CHRIS ELLIOT
D.O.B. //
P.O.B. //

NEAREST RELATIVE: CLAIRE PHELPS
LOCATOR NO.: EKLO: GRIXHLIQU: 8.364
PAY GRADE: G3-4L (TSP++HELTE
LAST SECURITY DISC UPDATE: 01.02.93
TRAINING AGENT: NIGEL HSYON

ACTOR PROFILE

Mission: Implausible

Sure *Mission: Impossible* is unrealistic. A helicopter flies through a tunnel, for crying out loud! But it is not the aeronautical gymnastics that bother cybercitizens most. It's that email, that damned email, in which secrets are revealed and malevolent plots are foiled. A writer to Harp on *Mission: Impossible*, a site devoted to debunking the big-budget moneymaker, expresses it best: "It's impossible to have a space in an email address, but Max@Book Of Job seemed to be receiving quite a bit of email."

Harp on Mission: Impossible

WEB http://www.lungfish.com/alteregos/velcro/soforth/harponmi.html

Administrator cannot read your mail."). There is a small fee for the software.
WEB http://www.compulink.co.uk/~net-services/jd.htm

▶ **Mixmaster List** Automatically generated list of mixmasters, including latency and average upload time for each. The list is updated twice a month.
WEB http://kiwi.cs.berkeley.edu/mixmaster-list.html

▶ **Mixmaster Remailers** Also known as Remail, the Next Generation; mixmaster remailers use advanced techniques to render conventional methods of tracing remailed messages useless. This mixmaster information page not only links users to mixmaster FAQs and servers, but also provides a forum for the system's critics.
WEB http://www.stack.urc.tue.nl/~galactus/remailers/index-mix.html

▶ **Private Idaho: Internet Email Privacy** Download the latest version of Private Idaho, a Windows tool which simplifies the happy union of PGP and anonymous remailers.
WEB http://www.eskimo.com/~joelm/pi.html

And the Web? How can I visit sites invisibly?

As explained earlier, your email address is publicly available on the Internet, as is your real name, although some servers give you the option of making it private. Your address and telephone number are easily obtainable, too, unless you take active steps to prevent their publication. There are ways, however, that you can surf the Web anonymously.

The truth is in the mix
http://www.stack.urc.tue.nl/~galactus/remailers/index-mix.html

► **The Anonymizer** The Myth: "On the Internet, nobody knows you're a dog." The Reality: They not only know you're a dog, but also your pedigree, collar size, and favorite biscuit flavor. As the Anonymizer is quick to point out, most sites keep a record of your visits, so someone out there knows where you're going online, and how often. But a visit to this site each time you log on will fix that, allowing you to surf the Web without revealing any personal information.
WEB http://www.anonymizer.com

Pull Out Your Finger

Fingering, we should now be clear in our minds, is no more a safe sex alternative than it is a method for learning the bassoon. In fact, for the privacy seeker, there's nothing safe about it. Your finger program is an easy way for other users to access your user name and address, and to see whether or not you are currently logged on. For many people, the open-book existence is a desirable state. A finger can act as a business card, a pithy advertisement for services rendered, akin to a user profile on the commercial services. For others, however, being fingered is a nuisance and an invasion of privacy. Your long-lost friend, Bernie, may use your email address to call in that decade-old poker debt. Your ability to delete your finger file varies from one service provider to another. You should contact your service administrator directly to review your options.

> **How Do I Keep Track of People Who are Fingering Me?** Unfortunately, it may not be possible, but this site will help you to the extent of your computer's ability.
> WEB http://www.ee.byu.edu/unix-faq/subsubsection3_6_7_l.html

Trash the Cache

The disk cache on your Internet browser automatically stores pages you have previously visited. This has the effect of removing the download time of pages you regularly visit. The flipside of this is that your boss or your cyber-savvy children, or anyone with the necessary (and not particularly advanced) skills, can dig into your system and find out where you have been wandering around the Web. But there are ways to take out the cache.

Frank is back in his Cube and all's right with the world
http://www.cloud9.net/~frankp/welcome.html

Location: http://www.cloud9.net/~frankp/welcome.html

Cube-Cam

➤ **MECCA Online Privacy Issues** "Do you re-member where you surfed last week? Your boss or your kids do!" No matter what the Netscape Handbook says, caches are not your friends, at least where privacy is concerned. The Michigan Electronic Communities of Concerned Adults explains the implications of cache files in great detail, and then tells you what to do about them.
WEB http://www.id.net/~mecca/privacy/yokl.html

Cut Your Cookies

Web sites can store information about you through the use of cookies. Don't let the precious name fool you; cookies are the privacy seeker's ultimate nemesis, and should be wiped out as soon as possible. You can delete your cookie file after each session, but a new one will be created for you each time you visit a site that wants to store information about you. The site then stores this information in a file called cookies.text on Windows, and MagicCookie on MacIntosh. These are standard text files, and are more than often stored in the same directory as you will find the Navigator program itself. Kill the Cookies and Deleting Cookies offer two methods for getting rid of the pests named for everybody's favorite junk food.

➤ **Deleting Cookies** A guide to the manual deletion of cookie files.
WEB http://ebweb.tuwien.ac.at/gnu-docs/elib/elib_29 .html#SEC3I

➤ **Kill the Cookie** An applet that automatically deletes the MagicCookie from the Preferences folder after each online session.
WEB http://micros.hensa.ac.uk/cgi-bin/msg2html /path=micros/mac/finder/g/gll9

COOKIE MONSTERS

"For those concerned with cookies and Netscape's treatment of them, Netscape has a new solution. In the older betas of Netscape 3.0, you were offered a choice where it would alert you before accepting a cookie. You could click Accept or Cancel to decide whether or not to let the web page write a cookie to your hard drive. Netscape has now fixed this problem. How? By no longer offering that option. Netscape 3.0 beta 5 automatically accepts all cookies, and there is no option to deny or turn them off. What a solution. Guess I'll have to go to the solutions suggested by others, making the file read-only, putting a directory with the same name, etc. No doubt the next version of Netscape will have the ability to change the file permissions and work around this. HEY NETSCAPE! NOT EVERYONE WANTS TO BE TRACKED!!!"

—from **alt.privacy**

> **Malcolm's Guide to Persistent Cookies** Know the enemy, and his PR campaign. Malcolm offers an optimistic view of cookies, claiming that their anti-security potential has been grossly exaggerated.
> WEB http://www.emf.net/~mal/cookiesinfo.html

> **NSClean** At any of these sites, you can access a free demo of a $20 program which rubs out Netscape's cookies, cache files and the even more notorious history databases.
> WEB http://www.simtel.net/pub/simtelnet/win3/inet /ns-demo2.zip •http://www.shareware.com
> URL ftp://ftp.simtel.net/pub/simtelnet/win3/inet /ns-demo2.zip

Don't Eat the Applets

It's official. The cuter the name, the more insidious the application. You've been cautioned about cookies; now, arm yourself against the destructive power of applets. An applet is a Java program that is run from inside a Web browser. A hostile applet is any applet which exploits or monopoloizes your system's resources in an inappropriate manner, thus compromising your security. Hostile applets are easy to write and pose serious threats to online commerce.

> **Frequently Asked Questions - Applet Security** JavaSoft answers the charges against them in this FAQ.
> WEB http://java.sun.com/sfaq/index.html

> **Hostile Applets Home Page** This page invites you, at your own risk, to download some hostile applets. See what all the fuss is about, and then follow links to resources that help you deal with them.

ROGUE APPLETS?

"Can an applet start another program on the client?"

"No, applets loaded over the Net are not allowed to start programs on the client. That is, an applet that you visit can't start some rogue process on your PC. In UNIX terminology, applets are not allowed to exec or fork processes. In particular, this means that applets can't invoke some program to list the contents of your file system, and it means that applets can't invoke System.exit() in an attempt to kill your web browser. Applets are also not allowed to manipulate threads outside the applet's own thread group."

—from **Frequently Asked Questions—Applet Security**

Location: http://biznow.com/sammy.htm

Welcome to Sammy's Souvlaki!

12:29:59 PM

The lunchtime rush for a Sammy Special
http://biznow.com/sammy.htm

WEBhttp://www.math.gatech.edu/~mladue/Hostile
Applets.html

➤ **Java Security: From HotJava to Netscape and Beyond** This paper exposes numerous un-truths behind Java's claim to security.
WEBhttp://www.cs.princeton.edu/sip/pub/secure96
.html

Get Unlisted

People-search sites on the Internet, such as Yahoo's People Search, allow you to delete your information from their archives. The process is simple, but somewhat time con-suming; you have to send your request to each service. Instructions for doing just that can be found at the following areas of these Web sites, which have been reviewed earlier in the book:

➤ **Bigfoot FAQ**
WEBhttp://www.Bigfoot.com/faqs2.htm#removal

➤ **FourII White Pages Directory FAQ**
WEB http://www.fourII.com/cgi-bin/SledMain?Iside
_HM_InfoDir.html#FAQ26

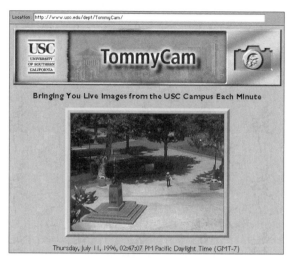

Tommy Trojan never moves, no matter how long you watch him
http://www.usc.edu/dept/TommyCam

➤ Internet Address Finder FAQ
WEB http://www.iaf.net/faq.htm#remove

➤ People Search
WEB http://phone.yahoo.com

➤ Switchboard
WEB http://www.switchboard.com/policy.htm

Erase your past
Your old Usenet posts may come back to haunt you. Archives such as DejaNews and Alta Vista allow others to access your past posts, and, by extension, your email address. However, it is possible to conceal your address and even to delete old posts from the archive. For more information, check out the DejaNews FAQ or contact DejaNews directly (comments@dejanews.com) to request that your old posts be removed.

➤ Deja News FAQ
WEB http://www.dejanews.com/help/dnfaq.html#content

encryption

I. **Just how good is "Pretty Good Privacy" and where can I get some?**
Downloads, detailed instructions, FAQs, and sources.

II. **I've encrypted my email, but what about the data on my hard disk? Can I encrypt that, too?**
Download the programs that hide the work for you.

III. **Where can I learn steganography as something to fall back on?**
Not the art of writing in shorthand, steganography is, in fact, the technology of hiding files inside of other files.

I want to know the code

g7$&)JIjoN9L

The above encrypted message reveals a fail-proof get-rich-quick scheme. Maybe. If you only knew how to *decrypt* it. To turn the gibberish back into something readable, you need the *key*, or the decoding system.

Like sending an unsigned love letter to the object of your desires, anonymous remailers allow you a certain amount of blameless, irresponsible luxury. However, unless you're simply deriding the denizens of your least favorite newsgroup, anonymity is simply not enough. True security is achieved through a combination of remailing and encryption.

Don't let the syllables scare you; encryption is basically a fancy word for code, and, let's face it, code is fun. Cereal and toy companies know it—hence decoder rings and magic ink—and so does the government—hence the losing battle against certain encryption programs. To encrypt is to hide information behind a façade of gibberish, as in the above example.

If Bob sends an encrypted email to his Cousin Fred in Reno, Fred needs Bob's key to decrypt the nonsensical code. Yet if Bob sends Fred his key over the unprotected channels of the Internet, he undermines the very security he was trying to protect in the first place.

Enter *public key cryptography*. This system solves the Bob and Fred dilemma by giving each user two keys, one to encrypt, the other

PGP IN THE U.S.A.

"What does 'international' mean? Who may use it?"

"PGP 2.6.3i was put together to provide an alternative to the American versions of PGP, which are distributed by MIT and contain a number of restrictions that are not relevant for users outside the USA. In general, 'international' means 'non-US,' i.e. it may be used by anyone except those who live in the US."

"Why isn't it official? Is it illegal to use?"

"PGP 2.6.3i is perfectly legal to use provided that you:

1. Don't live in a country where encryption is illegal (such as France, Russia, Iran, Iraq or China).

Award-winning concealment
http://www.primenet.com/~wprice/cdisk.html

to decrypt the data. One is open to the public; the other a jealously guarded secret. Now, if Bob wants to send an encrypted email to Cousin Fred, he must first find out out Fred's *public key* and use it to encrypt the data. Fred then decrypts the data with his *private key*, never having compromised its sanctity. Much to its intense chagrin, the government itself cannot read Bob and Fred's encrypted email.

In 1991, Phil Zimmerman released—free of charge—his easy-to-use public-key encryption program, PGP (Pretty Good Privacy). Displeasure became outright hostility as the government saw encryption go from a hi-tech luxury to a commonplace reality. As a result, encryption has become one of the most widely debated topics in cyberspace, spawning the sharpest government/private citizen schism since the Stamp Act. Furthermore, because encryption programs are classified as munitions, they are subject to export restrictions under the International Traffic in Arms Regulations (ITAR). United States suppliers who make strong encryption programs available to non-U.S. citizens over the Internet may be punishable by a fine of up to $1 million and 10 years in prison.

2. Are not physically inside the USA.

3. Make sure that you don't download a copy of PGP that is physically inside the USA. If you get it from the PGPi download page, you should be on the safe side.

"The reason why PGP 2.6.3i is not official, is that is was based on source code that was once illegaly exported from the USA. However, once the program has been exported, anyone may use it freely. Phil Zimmermann, the original author of PGP, has issued a public statement on PGP 2.6.i (the predecessor to PGP 2.6.3i), which is as close to an endorsement that he could possibly get without incriminating himself."

—from **FAQ About the International PGP Versions**

Zimmerman has become an Internet celebrity and his PGP the de facto encryption standard, even while he is still wrapped up in legal battles regarding export control policies. Obtaining PGP is easy, as is generating public and private keys. Once you've read the FAQs and downloaded the appropriate material, you too can use PGP in conjunction with remailing to become a truly private cybercitizen.

Just how good is "Pretty Good Privacy" and where can I get some?

MIT runs the official PGP site for the U.S. and Canada. Read at least one FAQ first, and then go to the site for the goods. You'll need to jump through some hoops to verify your North American residency, but it's a small price to pay for a free and essentially foolproof program. Upon obtaining PGP, you'll need to decide your key size. Size equals security, but be careful not to make your keys too big, or users with versions of PGP that don't support large key sizes may run into problems. A pretty good standard size is 1024 bits.

"Size equals security, but be careful not to make your keys too big."

▶ **Beginner's Guide to PGP and Internet Privacy**
Beginning with a list of useful terms and definitions, this FAQ is clear and easy to follow. Its author includes his email address, selflessly offering to answer the questions of the hopelessly confused.
WEB http://www.arc.unm.edu/~drosoff/pgp/pgp.html

cryptonomics

I. I'm shopping for spy gear online and I don't want anyone to know. How do I shop covertly?

The answer is digital cash.

II. Who ensures secure transactions on the Internet?

Virtual banks to help you spend your virtual cash safely.

Isn't that what killed Superman?

At www.spystuff.com, they do accept American Express. And MasterCard. And, for that matter, Visa. Shopping online may seem like the only alternative for the spy who wants to keep his operations undercover. After all, what good is that heavy-duty surveillance equipment when your target knows exactly what's in store?

Yet before you begin ordering spy cameras and optical night vision goggles from the comfort of your home computer, consider the following scenario from the annals of online commerce history: In December, 1994, "Trieu Le" posted advertisements in misc .forsale.computers, listing a variety of reasonably priced computer hardware and software. The approximately 50 users who responded and agreed to pre-pay for the merchandise received empty boxes in the mail. The return address was a Mailboxes, etc. store.

Although this sad tale features extremely naive buyers and a particularly wily con artist, even the circumspect online shopper can run into problems. From well-disguised scams to hackers after credit card numbers, the cybermall is more perilous than a Barney's warehouse sale. The con artists should be avoided altogether, of course, but there are safe, private ways to to purchase goods online from legitimate sources. This section will inform you of the specific risks to the online shopper, and help you protect yourself againt them.

CRYPTO- NOMICS 101

digital cash: Electronic money exchange involving neither a coin nor paper transaction

identified digital cash: Contains the identity of the person who withdrew the money from the bank. Can be tracked by the bank.

anonymous digital cash: Anonymous digital cash is like real cash in that it leaves no paper trail after its withdrawal.

double spending: Counterfeiting digital cash by copying bits once they've been withdrawn. Magic Money, the cypherpunk digital cash offering, eradicates double spending potential by requiring communication between client and server during each transaction.

The virtual bank for the virtual shopper
http://www.fv.com

I'm shopping for spy gear online and I don't want anyone to know. How do I shop covertly?

The key to secure transactions online is digital cash, electronic currency that depends upon the union of cryptography and economics. Developed by David Chaum, founder of Dig-iCash, digital cash provides users with the anonymity of paper currency, along with the security afforded by public-key cryptography.

➤ **Digicrime, Inc.** The brilliance of this "full service computer hacking organization" is that it satirizes Internet vulnerabilities while imparting very real information. The employees of Digicrime find exploitable weaknesses, invent accompanying scams, and taunt users with the lucrative-sounding, all-too-real possibilities.
WEB http://www.digicrime.com

➤ **Digital Cash and Monetary Freedom** Learn the differences between true digital cash and "mere encrypted credit card schemes."
WEB http://info.isoc.org/HMP/PAPER/I36/abst.html

➤ **Digital Cash Mini-FAQ** Answers the questions: How is digital cash possible? Are there different kinds of digital cash, and what is the double-spending problem? WEB http://ganges.cs.tcd.ie/mepeirce/Project/Mlists/minifaq.html

➤ **e-payment@cc.bellcore.com** A mailing list concerned with electronic payment protocols. EMAIL Majordomo@cc.bellcore.com ✍ *Type in message body:* subscribe e-payment

➤ **EEF Privacy/Online Commerce Archives** The advocacy group's collection of articles on secure transactions. WEB http://www.eff.org/pub/Privacy/Digital_money

➤ **Electronic Payment Schemes** With its "three-layered model" for comparing payment schemes, this paper is a bit on the verbose side, but its listing of resources is extensive, and it's nice to know that someone out there is theorizing about all this stuff. WEB http://www.w3.org/pub/WWW/Payments/roadmap.html

Sammy doesn't accept digital cash
http://biznow.com/sammy.htm

➤ **Information on Web Transaction Security** This site features information on secure transactions, some of which is highly technical.
WEB http://www.w3.org/pub/WWW/Security/#wts

➤ **Network Payment Mechanisms and Digital Cash** Links to articles, resources, and mailing lists.
WEB http://ganges.cs.tcd.ie/mepeirce/project.html

➤ **www-buyinfo Mailing List Home Page** Subscribe to this mailing list devoted to the discussion of Web transactions, or read through the archives.
WEB http://www.research.att.com/www-buyinfo

Who ensures secure transactions on the Internet?

These sites have payment schemes designed for safe buying and selling on the Net.

➤ **BankNet** A U.K.-based online transaction service offering a number of payment options.
WEB http://mkn.co.uk/bank

➤ **Clickshare** Clickshare may be used to track and monitor your online digital cash purchases.
WEB http://www.clickshare.com/clickshare

➤ **DigiCash** DigiCash is the company that produces ecash, one of the very first digital cash currencies. You withdraw ecash from a bank and store it on your local computer, spending at any online shop which accepts ecash. Your ecash is protected by public key digital signature

MY MOMMA DIDN'T RAISE NO DUMMY!

• **Consumer Protection** The Internet is an exciting new medium for the pyramid schemer and weight loss vendor alike. You may think you're too smart to fall into a charlatan's clutches, but a little extra prudence never hurt anybody. Visit this site to read, "Online Scams: Roadblocks on the Information Superhighway." If nothing else, you can laugh at the stupidity of the credulous dupes who sold their kids into slavery for the chance to get rich quick with "no loss possible."
WEB http://www.isa.net/project-open/conpro.html

THE ONLINE 5-FINGER DISCOUNT

"Welcome to The Internet Shoplifting Network.

"Wish you could afford those Gucci loafers? Like to shop from the privacy and comfort of your own home? Tired of paying full price for your Internet purchases? You should try our Internet Shoplifting Service! We currently offer this service for the theft of both information services and goods. For information services we simply retrieve the information and pass it on to you. For goods we use someone else's credit card number and drop ship them to an address that you specify. Our fee is currently being waived during this promotional period. As of the first of the year, we will begin charging a mere 2% of the original cost of the item (shipping is extra on goods). You save 98% on all goods and information services!"

—from **Digicrime, Inc.**

techniques, and by a password known only to you. Furthermore, your anonymity is protected by ecash, because you need not reveal your identity to the payee.
WEB http://digicash.support.nl

▶ **First Virtual** This Internet payment scheme boasts simplicity. When you shop, give a Virtual PIN number to the seller rather than a credit card. First virtual will then send you an email to confirm the purchase. The system's advantage is the negation of the double-spending threat.
WEB http://www.fv.com

▶ **NetCash** NetCash uses identified online electronic cash, although there are some mechanisms through which coins can be exchanged to allow some anonymity. NetCash is highly secure and scalable against the threat of double-spending.
WEB http://ganges.cs.tcd.ie/mepeirce/Project /Oninternet/netcash.ps

▶ **PayMe: Secure Cash Payment for WWW Resources** The most secure payment scheme for the Internet is one in which the money being spent cannot be linked with their owner. PayMe is just such a system, combining the best features of ecash and NetCash to achieve the latest and safest in online payment protocol.
WEB http://www.w3.org/pub/Conferences/WWW4 /Papers/228

▶ **Secure Electronic Transactions** Providing secure electronic transactions through the use of bank cards.
WEB http://www.visa.com/cgi-bin/vee/sf/set/intro.html

security

I. I'm feeling insecure. What will make me feel better?

If it's your computer that has the problem, maybe all you need is some good advice on securing the goods.

II. It's just me and my PC. How can I make sure that we're safe?

A good password and filewipe utilities will help you sleep at night.

III. My network is vulnerable from the inside and out. How can I keep it free from unwanted attention?

Firewalls, Kerberos, and SATAN can help. If all else fails, there are people you can call.

How do I keep the bad stuff out and the good stuff in?

Securing your personal hardware and software can be as simple as locking the door when you leave your apartment. The appropriate security level for you depends upon the likelihood that someone would want what you've got. The first level of defense is a good password, and, for some people, that's enough.

When a computer joins a network, security is far more complicated. Computers connected in a network communicate with each other through a language or protocol called TCP/IP. Most office and institution computers have a direct connection to one another. Rather than communicating via modem, they are connected by wires, usually Ethernet cables. The network's vulnerability to external factors is exacerbated by the potential for internal human error or intentional sabotage. Codifying the security measures on the inside is as important as safeguarding the outward lines of defense. In this section, you'll learn how to protect your personal computer and your network from internal and external threats.

RISK FACTORS

"Exactly what security risks are we talking about?"

"There are basically four overlapping types of risk:
1. Private or confidential documents stored in the Web site's document tree falling into the hands of unauthorized individuals.

2. Private or confidential information sent by the remote user to the server (such as credit card information) being intercepted.

I'm feeling insecure. What will make me feel better?

It should come as no surprise that people on the Internet are talking about computer and network security, nor should it come as a surprise that the language they use is often highly technical. Sites listed here use straightforward language.

➤ **alt.security** "There's no such thing as an uncrackable system," writes one alt.security regular, spawning a debate that threads its way from post to post. Others write in to praise or critique the latest technology.
USENET alt.security

➤ **comp.security.misc** For some reason, tensions run high in this newsgroup as users argue passionately about security issues. Everything from the latest in cryptography to the sanctity of passwords evokes impassioned debate and the occasional hurling of epithets.
USENET comp.security.misc

➤ **Computer Security FAQ** An FAQ which answers questions frequently asked in the newsgroups alt.security, comp.security.misc, and comp.security.unix.
WEB http://www.cis.ohio-state.edu/hypertext/faq/usenet/security-faq/faq.html

➤ **Netsurfer Focus: Computer and Network Security** A comprehensive, well-organized guide to security from the writers of *Netsurfer Digest*. Beginning with the premise that "the only safe computer is a dead computer," the writers break it down with a minimum of extraneous chatter, one security measure at a time.
WEB http://www.netsurf.com/nsf/v0l/0l/nsf.0l.0l.html#scl

➤ **NSCA InfoSecurity Forum** While the commercial services don't exactly yield a wealth of privacy and security information, the NSCA Security Forum proves the exception to the rule. The NSCA is

```
3. Information
   about the Web
   server's host
   machine leaking
   through, giving
   outsiders ac-
   cess to data
   that can poten-
   tially allow
   them to break
   into the host.

4. Bugs that allow
   outsiders to
   execute com-
   mands on the
   server's host
   machine, allow-
   ing them to
   modify and/or
   damage the sys-
   tem. This in-
   cludes "denial
   of service" at-
   tacks, in which
   the attackers
   pummel the ma-
   chine with so
   many requests
   that it is ren-
   dered effec-
   tively use-
   less."

—from WWW Security
   FAQ
```

What's Wrong With This Picture?

Oh No, Net Again!

The compilers of Stupid Computer Tricks, a Web site devoted to remarking on the flawed use of computers in movies, point out one overlooked solution to that pesky matter of national security in *The Net*: "Most of the chase was started after the Mozart's Ghost Web page is pulled up. There is a pi symbol in the bottom right-hand corner that runs something bad—the Gatekeeper backdoor. So why doesn't anybody just open the HTML file and delete the image and the HREF tag?"

The Net
WEB http://www.holly
wood.com/movies/bsnet

Stupid Computer Tricks
WEB http://www.creative
loafing.com/staff/howard
.fore/stupid/

dedicated to helping you solve your security problems, and claims to have assembled a support team of experts to answer security-related questions relating to info. The message boards are an outlet for discussion and technical advice, while the libraries contain an incredible collection of documents on security management and technology.
COMPUSERVE *go* security

▷ **WWW Security FAQ** This document is an invaluable resource for anyone who is willing to read about the issue from beginning to end.
WEB http://www-genome.wi.mit.edu/WWW
/faqs/www-security-faq.html

It's just me and my PC. How can I make sure that we're safe?

A good password, a filewipe utility and you're good to go, assuming you don't leave your laptop out in the sun too long.

Passwords
Your maiden name is too obvious. Everybody in the office knows your dog's name (Mr. Snuggly Bear) and his nickname (Pookums). But if you choose something too obscure, how will you ever remember it? Believe it or not, there are people out there who covet the special word that is near and dear to your heart. Crackers can use your password to send emails, post to newsgroups in your name, and leave security holes in your account. This collection of sites offer advice on choosing, using, and not losing your password.

➤ **Computer Passwords** Good passwords, bad passwords, and what to do if you forget your password, or want to change it.
WEB http://lime.weeg.uiowa.edu/departments/oit /weeg-docs/passwords.html

➤ **Privacy Begins with Your Passphrase** "Use the first line of a song or poem," and other sound advice.
URL ftp://ftp.crl.com/users/ro/smart/TFP/passphrase .html

Deleting Files

Your boss criticizes your wardrobe and, in a fit of rage, you decide to quit. Your resignation letter, replete with epithets, threats and impious language, seems like a masterpiece in the heat of the moment. But after a good night's sleep, you realize the error of your ways, and you delete the file from your office computer. Is it gone? Nope. Your angry cussing is still alive and kicking on the hard

When it comes to online security, three heads are better than one
http://www.ov.com/misc/krb-faq.html

Location: http://www.ov.com/misc/krb-faq.html

Kerberos Users' Frequently Asked Questions

Kerberos; also spelled Cerberus. n. The watch dog of Hades, whose duty it was to guard the entrance--against whom or what does not clearly appear; . . . it is known to have had three heads. . .
        -Ambrose Bierce, The Enlarged Devil's Dictionary

disk, easily recovered by relatively simple un-delete programs. If you really want to eradicate a file, you must overwrite it using a file wipe utility.

> **File Wipe Utilities** This site contains information on file wipers and links to a number of good ones.
> WEB http://www.stack.urc.tue.nl/~galactus/remailers /index-wipe.html

> **Mark Andreas Home Page** Visit this guy's home page to download the latest version of his wipeutil.zip for DOS.
> WEB http://www.sky.net/~voyageur

My network is vulnerable from the inside and out. How can I keep it free from unwanted attention?

You know you're having a bad day when some kid with a laptop breaks into your company's system, steals the secrets of your success, and sells them to the competition. Ominous names notwithstanding, firewalls, Kerberos, and SATAN may very well be your ticket to security heaven.

Firewalls

When you connect your computer to the Internet, you are opening it up to a world of potential intruders. A little paranoia goes a long way. Firewalls monitor traffic from the inside and out, ensuring that only selected communications can move over the network threshold in either direction. Actually, a firewall is basically a pair of mechanisms; one which exists to block traffic, the other to let it in. Firewalls are custom made, so that the access

---

"WHAT" IS THE PASSWORD

"Poor Passwords

"Don't choose a password contained in English or foreign language dictionaries, spelling lists, or other lists of words. Nor should you use as a password a word from the dictionary, preceded or followed by a single character. These can be cracked. It's generally a good idea not to use names of any kind, including: Your login name in any form (as is, reversed, capitalized, doubled, etc.). Your first or last name in any form. Your spouse's or child's name. Don't use your phone number. Don't use other information easily obtained about you. Don't use simple keyboard patterns such as "qwerty" or "12345678." Don't use well known phrase mnemonics such as ROYGBIV

Location: http://ciac.llnl.gov/ciac/ToolsUnixNetMon.html#Courtney

Courtney

Courtney is the work of CIAC. It monitors the network and identifies the source machines of SATAN probes/attacks. Courtney receives input from tcpdump counting the number of new services a machine originates within a certain time window. If one machine connects to numerous services within that time window, Courtney identifies that machine as a potential SATAN host.

DOWNLOAD

Courtney: Smarter than the average toddler
http://ciac.llnl.gov/ciac/ToolsUnixNetMon.html#Courtney

control policy for a particular network depends upon the level of security desired by that network. A strict policy might be one which allows only the inflow of email.

➤ **A Toolkit and Methods for Internet Firewalls** A firewall toolkit designed to be used with a host-based security policy.
WEB http://www.tis.com/Home/NetworkSecurity /Firewalls/Usenix.html

➤ **drawbridge (IP bridging filter)** Keeps invaders out of the cybercastle.
URL ftp://net.tamu.edu/pub/security/TAMU

➤ **FAQ—Firewalls** What a firewall is, and what it isn't. They protect against unauthorized logins, not viruses.
WEB http://www.v-one.com/pubs/fw-faq/faq.htm

➤ **Firewall Toolkit** A freeware toolkit for the building and maintenance of Internet firewalls.
URL ftp://ftp.tis.com/pub/firewalls/toolkit

➤ **Firewalls and Internet Security** Many firewalls feature packet filtering mechanisms. "What's that?" you might well ask. Ac-

(colors of the rainbow), EGBDF (notes on the musical staff), or WYSIWYG (what you see is what you get). Don't use a password of all digits, or all the same letter. This significantly decreases the search time for a cracker. Don't choose two short words and concatenate them together. Even two words with a punctuation character between them can be cracked. While at this University, do not choose our team names or host names as passwords. For example, do not use Hawkeye, Herky, Blue, Umaxa, Umaxc, or VAXA. Also avoid the use of "password" or "secret" as your password. Don't store both your project number and password in an IBM JCL file kept online."

—from **Computer Passwords**

cording to this site, it's the fancy term for the process by which the firewall decides what can come into the network (email, for example), and what cannot (telnet addresses, maybe).

WEB http://www.willamette.edu/~dlabar/firewall.html

➤ **Index—The Rotherwick Firewall Resource** A listing of firewall resources around the Internet, including shareware and freeware packages.

WEB http://www.zeuros.co.uk/firewall

➤ **Keeping the Visigoths Out** *PC Week*'s guide to the best and brightest firewalls.

WEB http://www.ziff.com/~pcweek/netweek/jan_1995 /rev_ttech_0123.html

➤ **Socks (generic proxy server)** SOCKS is a networking proxy mechanism that enables hosts on one side of SOCKS server to gain full access to hosts on the other side of the server without requiring a direct IP connection. It works by redirecting connection requests from hosts away from the

Better the devil you know
http://www.fish.com/satan

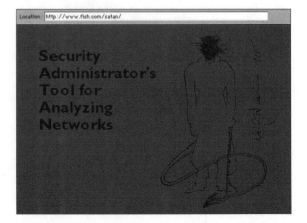

Location: http://www.fish.com/satan/

Security Administrator's Tool for Analyzing Networks

other host, and to a SOCKS server, which authenticates and authorizes the request, establishes a proxy connection and passes data back and forth.

URL ftp://ftp.nec.com/pub/security/socks.cstc

Kerberos, the three-headed hound from hell

Kerberos is a security package which protects networks from internal threats through the cryptographic protection of passwords and other sensitive information. If you try to login to another host in your network, Kerberos will ensure that you have the proper authority to do so. Named for the mythical hound who guards the gates of Hades, Kerberos effectively manufactures secret keys to ensure proper user identification. It can also be used for local password verification, such as at individual workstations in an office, although not without some difficulty.

> "**Kerberos is named for the mythical hound who guards the gates of Hades.**"

⮞ **Kerberos (Unix)** The MIT distribution site for the Unix version.
   URL ftp://athena-dist.mit.edu/pub/kerberos

⮞ **Kerberos (Unix, Mac, Windows)** Cygnus Network Security uses Kerberos to guard system security, installing a secure sign on system and password verification protocol.
   WEB http://www.cygnus.com/data/cns.html

⮞ **Kerberos Users' Frequently Asked Questions** Cogently written and especially useful for explaining the different versions of the

program and how they might be useful.
WEB http://www.ov.com/misc/krb-faq.html

SATAN (Security Administrator Tool for Analyzing Networks)

For the system administrators of the world, hell is a vulnerable computer. SATAN is a tool that probes for and analyzes system vulnerabilities. Although not the first tool of its kind, SATAN is unique for its ease, and for the extensive documentation it returns on the weaknesses and how they can be fixed. Of course SATAN can also be used by crackers to probe potential victims for weaknesses. The following sites talk about SATAN distribution and use, and about the potential for misuse.

▶ **Courtney** A tool for monitoring SATAN probes and attacks.
WEB http://ciac.llnl.gov/ciac/ToolsUnixNetMon.html #Courtney

▶ **Detailed Review of SATAN** This paper examines SATAN's potential use by crackers, and how the process can be countered.
WEB http://ciac.llnl.gov/ciac/notes/Notes07.shtml

▶ **Internet Security Systems** Like SATAN, this program promises to "find your network security holes before the hackers do."
WEB http://iss.net/iss/scanner.html

▶ **SATAN** Includes a short FAQ and guides users to distribution sites for the program.
WEB http://www.fish.com/satan

▶ **SPI** Performs searches for security holes "at the touch of a button."
WEB http://ciac.llnl.gov/cstc/CSTCProducts.html#spi

WHAT SHOULD I DO IF MY NETWORK IS UNDER ATTACK?

• **What to Do if Your Site Has Been Compromised** First, don't panic. Second, refer to this FAQ, which will show you how to trace the intruder and prevent further break-ins.
WEB http://www.cis.ohio -state.edu/hypertext/faq /usenet/computer-security /compromise-faq/faq.html

• **CERT—United States** Third, and only if all else fails, call the Computer Emergency Response Team for expert guidance. Hotline number: 412-268-7090.
WEB http://www.cert.org

appendix

I. **People finders**

II. **Employee screening services**

III. **Full-service P.I.s**

IV. **Credit report services**

V. **Corporate spies for hire**

PEOPLE FINDERS

- **B. W. Griffin**
  WEB http://www.cpgs.com/prieye

- **Capital Finders**
  WEB http://www.cache.net/finders

- **CIS Locator**
  WEB http://www.cistx.com

- **Cox Information Services**
  WEB http://www.coxfindmfast.com

- **DATATRAC Search and Locate Services**
  WEB http://www.commpass.net/datatrac

- **Detective Alvie L. Davidson**
  WEB http://www.cris.com/~genie4u /detective.html

- **Find A Friend**
  WEB http://www.ais.net/findafriend

- **Finders Seekers Investigations**
  WEB http://www.finders-seekers.com

- **Harvey E. Morse/Locaters International**
  WEB http://www.netctrl.com/locaters

- **International Genealogical Search Inc.**
  WEB http://www.heirsearch.com

- **International Tracing Services**
  WEB http://www.skiptrace.com

- **Locators, Inc.**
  WEB http://ourworld.compuserve.com /homepages/locator

- **MetroNet**
  WEB http://www.jmg.gu.se/Nora_Paul /cardirec.htm#Met

- **People Finders Search Services**
  WEB http://pages.prodigy.com/mikep /search.htm

- **Safelink Inc.**
  WEB http://home.earthlink.net/~toptech /wpdocs/safelink.htm

- **Seekers of the Lost**
  WEB http://www.seeklost.com

- **Shadow Trackers**
  WEB http://idibbs.com/user/shadowtr /top.htm

- **Snow, Wayne**
  WEB http://www.greatbasin.net /~windsong/pef.html

- **Tracer Net**
  WEB http://ddi.digital.net/~harris

EMPLOYEE SCREENING SERVICES

- **Accurate Data Service**
  WEB http://www.acudata.com

- **Adrem Profiles, Inc.**
  WEB http://www.adpro.com

- **Alexander Information Group**
  WEB http://www.alexinfogp.com

- **American Tenant Screen**
  WEB http://www.pond.com/~fegely
  /atshome.htm

- **Avert**
  WEB http://www.avert.com

- **Background Research International**
  WEB http://www.investigator.com/bri

- **Background Verification Service**
  WEB http://www.mountain.net/hp/mar-
  com/hitec.htm

- **Bearak Reports**
  WEB http://www.bearak.com

- **Bishops Services, Inc.**
  WEB http://www.bishops-services-inc
  .com

- **CivicLink**
  WEB http://www.ameritech.com:1080
  /civiclink

- **CMI**
  WEB http://www.trcone.com/cmi.html

- **Consolidated Verification Services**
  WEB http://www.employeescreen.com

- **DataQuest**
  WEB http://www.nmia.com/~search
  /dataques.html

- **The Detective Information Network**
  WEB http://www.sni.net/din

- **DocuSearch**
  WEB http://www.docusearch.com
  /search.html

- **Franklin Information Group, Inc.**
  WEB http://www.figroup.com

- **Hi-Tec Info Resources**
  WEB http://www.hitecinfo.com

- **HITEC Info Resources**
  WEB http://www.hitecinfo.com/index.htm

- **Hogan Information Services**
  WEB http://www.hoganinfo.com

- **HRIS, Incorporated**
  WEB http://www.digisell.com/HRIS

- **Infinity Information Network**
  WEB http://www.smartpages.com
  /infinityinfo

- **Infinity Information Network**
  WEB http://synergy.smartpages.com
  /infinityinfo

EMPLOYEE SCREENING SERVICES

- **InfoHawks**
  WEB http://www.izad.com/infohawks

- **InformationForBusiness**
  WEB http://www.info4business.com

- **Informus Pre-Employment Screening**
  WEB http://www.informus.com

- **The Integrity Center**
  WEB http://www.integctr.com/Welcome.html

- **Intellichoice, Inc.**
  WEB http://www.atlantadirectory.com/findout

- **Interquest Information Services**
  WEB http://www.Interqst.com

- **Michael Moore Investigative Research**
  WEB http://world.std.com/~mmoore

- **National Locator & Data**
  WEB http://www.iu.net/hodges

- **Omni Partners**
  WEB http://www.omniscore.com

- **OmniSearch**
  WEB http://www.nvi.net/search/omnihome.html

- **Professional Information Services Network**
  WEB http://www.vii.com/~solgroup/credit

- **Sherlock**
  WEB http://www.ameri.com/sherlock/sherlock.htm

- **Slip-Tracer Information Services**
  WEB http://www.master.net/greenspot/sliptrac.html

- **!Solutions! Group**
  WEB http://www.vii.com/~solgroup/pro

- **StafTrack**
  WEB http://www.xtc.net/~staftrak

- **T-R Information Services**
  WEB http://www.shadow.net/~trinfo/asset.html

- **Tenant Screening Credit**
  WEB http://www.tsci.com

- **Variable Media Link, Inc.**
  WEB http://www.vmlink.com

- **World Information Network**
  WEB http://www.wininfo.com

FULL-SERVICE P.I.S

- **Agrue & Associates Investigations**
  WEB http://www.teleport.com/~pagrue
  /agrue.html

- **Alliance Investigations & Associates**
  WEB http://www.kern.com/alliance

- **Alpha Investigations**
  WEB http://www.1stresource.com/a
  /alpha

- **American Data Quest**
  WEB http://www.angelfire.com/free/adq
  .html

- **Amherst Group**
  WEB http://www.csz.com/amherst.html

- **Anderson Detective Agency**
  WEB http://acm.org/~GARLAND
  /gumshoe.html

- **AP Duli Investigations**
  WEB http://www.lm.com/~apduli

- **Armstrong & Associates**
  WEB http://www.mylink.net
  /~jarmstrong/arm.html

- **ATPI Investigations**
  WEB http://www.atpiinvestigations
  .com

- **Backstreet Investigators**
  WEB http://www.well.com/user
  /masonl23/bsiweb2.htm

- **Baxter and Associates**
  WEB http://www.baxtereyes.com

- **Blue Chip Investigations**
  WEB http://www.allworld.com/bluechip

- **The BodyGuard Page**
  WEB http://www.iapps.org

- **Brown Group, Inc.**
  WEB http://www.Private-Eye.com

- **The Cat Midwest**
  WEB http://www.spytaps.com/thecat

- **CFI Investigations**
  WEB http://turnpike.net/emporium/D
  /dcservice/wg/jamesv.htm

- **The Codex**
  WEB http://www.thecodex.com

- **Continental Investigative Services**
  WEB http://www.mja.net/continental

- **Corpa Investigations**
  WEB http://www.inforamp.net/~corpainv

- **Corvus Information & Investigation Services**
  WEB http://www.cyberline.com/corvus

- **Covert Services Investigation Agency**
  WEB http://www.knowledge.co.uk/xxx
  /covert

FULL-SERVICE P.I.S

- **Crummey Investigations**
  WEB http://www.iu.net/crummypi

- **Data Research, Inc.**
  WEB http://www.dataresearch.com

- **Decker-Neff Investigations, Inc.**
  WEB http://www.catol.com/decker-neff

- **Detective Information Network**
  WEB http://www.investigator.com/din

- **Dig Dirt Investigations**
  WEB http://www.pimall.com/moore
  /moore.html

- **Discreet Data Research**
  WEB http://www.discreetdata.com

- **Electronic Countermeasures Inc.**
  WEB http://www.t8000.com/eci/eci.htm

- **Emphasis Technography**
  WEB http://members.aol.com/tardieu
  /page/index.html

- **Eyewitness Investigations, Inc.**
  WEB http://www.eyewitness.com

- **FINE Investigations**
  WEB http://www.angelfire.com/free
  /jfine.html

- **Forbes International**
  WEB http://ids.net/~nepub/forbes
  /home.html

- **Global Investigation & Information Network, Inc.**
  WEB http://www.wta.com/giin

- **Golden West Group**
  WEB http://www.lynx.bc.ca./~goldenwest

- **Horizon Investigations**
  WEB http://emporium.turnpike.net
  /~megamall/horizon.htm

- **Illinois Counties Detective And Patrol Agency, Inc.**
  WEB http://www.cris.com/~jmgl3/ilcnty.htm

- **Infomax Investigative Services**
  WEB http://rlatham.trdigital.com
  /infomax.html

- **Investigation and Information Services**
  WEB http://www.tecs.com/invest

- **Investigative & Protective Services, Inc.**
  WEB http://pihome.com/ips/index.html

- **John Bullock and Company**
  WEB http://www.master.net/bullock

- **Klopper Investigations**
  WEB http://www.globaldomain.com
  /klopperpi

- **Larry Larsen Investigations**
  WEB http://www.earthlink.net
  /~larrylarsen

FULL-SERVICE P.I.S

- **Mandelbaum Edgerton Investigative Group, Inc.**
  WEB http://seamless.com/sleuth/index.html

- **MEC Investigations Division**
  WEB http://www.meconsult.co.uk/invest.htm

- **Metro Private Investigations, Inc.**
  WEB http://ro.com/~alegator

- **Mid-South Investigations**
  WEB http://www.pihome.com/msi

- **Midwest Investigative Services**
  WEB http://www.inf.net/~packy

- **Nationwide Investigations**
  WEB http://www.nwin.com

- **Network Investigations**
  WEB http://www.netinvest.com

- **New England Bureau of Investigations**
  WEB http://pages.prodigy.com/MA/detective/detective.html

- **P.D.I. Investigations**
  WEB http://www.pdi-web.com

- **Paragon Investigations, Inc.**
  WEB http://www.paragon-pi.com

- **Private Investigations**
  WEB http://www.syspac.com/~compuguy/private/privdick.html

- **Private Investigators**
  WEB http://www.pihome.com/investigators.html

- **Providence Investigations Ltd.**
  WEB http://www.king.igs.net/~providence

- **R & R Investigations Inc.**
  WEB http://www.rrinvestigations.com

- **Somers & Associates**
  WEB Somers & Associates

- **Sorensen & Sons Investigations**
  WEB http://www.sasipi.com

- **Special Investigations Unit**
  WEB http://www.siu.net

- **Specialized Investigations**
  WEB http://www.specialpi.com

- **Technical Surveillance Counter Measures (TSCM)**
  WEB http://www.tscm.com

- **Trakker & Associates Investigations**
  WEB http://iaswww.com/trakker.html

FULL-SERVICE P.I.S

- **United States Private Investigation Consultants Corp.**
  WEB http://www.privateyes.com

- **Virginia Snyder, Inc.**
  WEB http://www.ims-net.com/snyder

- **Vista, Inc.**
  WEB http://www.wwwpassport.net/vistapi

- **Ward & Associates**
  WEB http://www.wardinv.com

- **Wildman**
  WEB http://gn2.getnet.com/~wildman

- **Wood & Tait, Inc.**
  WEB http://www.maui.net/~berit/WoodTait.html

- **Zeiler & Associates**
  WEB http://www.cet.com/~kzeil

International

- **Agenzia Investigativa Internazionale**
  WEB http://hella.stm.it/market/detective/home.htm

- **Allied Investigators**
  WEB http://www.allied-investigators.co.uk

- **Intercom Detectives Internacionales**
  WEB http://www.interprov.com/nd/intercom

- **Interglobe Investigation Services**
  WEB http://www.jumppoint.com/interglobe/index.html

- **International Security & Detective Agency, Inc.**
  WEB http://www.pimall.com/isda/isda.html

- **Somers & Associates— International Investigators**
  WEB http://www.jax-inter.net/ispy

CREDIT REPORT SERVICES

- **American Credit Connection**
  WEB http://acc-empfacts.com

- **American Credit Counseling**
  WEB http://www.firstconsumer.com

- **Argus Information Service**
  WEB http://www.argus.co.il

- **Associated Credit Systems**
  WEB http://www.mind.net/acs

- **Credit Bureau Systems, Inc.**
  WEB http://www.creditbureau.com

- **Credit Research**
  WEB http://creditresearch.com

- **Creditreform**
  WEB http://www.creditreform.de/cred-itreform

- **Digital Matrix Systems, Inc.**
  WEB http://www.dms.net

- **Dynamic Business Information Ltd.**
  WEB http://www.dbinfo.co.uk/dbinfo

- **F&D Reports Online**
  WEB http://www.fdreports.com

- **First American Financial Corp.**
  WEB http://www.firstam.com

- **IRSC**
  WEB http://www.irsc.com

- **Mega Company Services Ltd.**
  WEB http://www.mega.co.uk

- **Mortgage Credit Reports**
  WEB http://www.webcreations.com/mcr

- **National Information Bureau, Ltd.**
  WEB http://www.nib.com

- **Northern California Credit Service**
  WEB http://www.nccredit.com

- **TRW Inc.**
  WEB http://www.trw.com

- **WWBC Credit Reporting Agencies**
  WEB http://www.teleport.com/~richh/agency.html

CORPORATE SPIES FOR HIRE

- **AKA Inc. Competitive Intelligence**
  WEB http://akainc.com

- **Allied Business Intelligence**
  WEB http://www.alliedworld.com/index.html

- **Alpha Investigations, Inc.**
  WEB http://lawinfo.com/biz/alpha.html

- **CombsMoorhead Associates**
  WEB http://homepage.interaccess.com/~cmainfo

- **Federal IT Competitive Intelligence**
  WEB http://www.caisisco.com/Infocenter.html

- **The Futures Group**
  WEB http://www.tfg.com

- **IBR International Business Research**
  WEB http://www.thevine.com/ibr

- **IceBreaker**
  WEB http://www.bdt.com/icemfg

- **InfoSearch**
  WEB http://www.switch.ch/is/index.htm

- **Intell Advantage**
  WEB http://members.gnn.com/Intel-lAdv/Home/iahome.htm

- **Intelligence Competitive Engine**
  WEB http://www.icemfg.com/icemfg

- **International Competitive Research**
  WEB http://infomanage.com/icr

- **International Research Group: Competitive Intelligence**
  WEB http://webcastl.com/irg/compete.htm

- **Investigative Resources International**
  WEB http://www.lainet.com/factfind

- **Kirk Tyson International Ltd.**
  WEB http://www.ktyson.com

- **Magian Solutions**
  WEB http://www.magian.com

- **NBR-Marketing/Competitive Intelligence**
  WEB http://www.nijenrode.nl/nbr/marketing/compi.html

- **Questel-Orbit**
  WEB http://www.questel.orbit.com/patents/readings/n_ci.html

- **T.R.A.D.E., Inc.**
  WEB http://www.tradeinfo.com

- **Vivamus Concepts**
  WEB http://www.vivamus.com/cointell.html

INDEX

RENNER LEARNING RESOURCE CENTER
ELGIN COMMUNITY COLLEGE
ELGIN, ILLINOIS 60123

WOLFF NEW MEDIA

Wolff New Media is one of the leading providers of information about the Net and the emerging Net culture. The company's NetBooks Series, presently at 17 titles—*Net-Guide, NetGames, NetChat, NetMoney, NetTrek, NetSports, Net-Tech, NetMusic, Fodor's NetTravel, NetTaxes, NetJobs, NetVote, NetMarketing, NetDoctor, NetStudy, NetCollege,* and *NetSpy*—will expand to more than 25 titles in 1996. This will include *NetKids, NetSci-Fi, NetShopping,* and *NetScreen.* The entire NetBooks Series (to date) is now available on the companion Web site YPN—Your Personal Net (http://www.ypn.com). And *Net Guide*—"the *TV Guide*® to Cyberspace," according to *Wired* magazine editor Louis Rossetto—is now a monthly magazine published by CMP Publications.

The company was founded in 1988 by journalist Michael Wolff to bring together writers, editors, and graphic designers to create editorially and visually compelling information products in books, magazines, and new media. Among the company's other projects are *Where We Stand—Can America Make It in the Global Race for Wealth, Health, and Happiness?* (Bantam Books), one of the most graphically complex information books ever to be wholly created and produced by means of desktop-publishing technology, and *Made in America?*, a four-part PBS series on global competitiveness, hosted by Labor Secretary Robert B. Reich.

The company frequently acts as a consultant to other information companies, including WGBH, Boston's educational television station; CMP Publications; and Time Warner, which it has advised on the development of Time's online business and the launch of its Web site, Pathfinder.

SONY THEATRES

"Judging by the thickness of the File on my desk I knew this case was going to be tough. But then again, you don't hire a Private Eye for the easy ones..."

We are looking for **SONY THEATRES** Mystery Shoppers.

provides the Mystery Shopper program as an opportunity to have our theatres evaluated. It's simple. You enroll to be a "shopper." Once enrolled you'll receive your free movie passes and concession coupons!

All you have to do is go to the Sony Theatre in your area and evaluate your movie going experience...

For more information on **SONY THEATRES MYSTERY SHOPPER** program click on theatres at http://www.sony.com or call 1-800-246-3519

Who are the most influential Asian Americans in the U.S.?

Who are the Asians making waves in Corporate America, in Cyberspace, in Hollywood?

What are the issues, challenges, and opportunities that face America's fastest-growing ethnic group?

Turn to A. Magazine for the answers! From politics to pop culture, from trends to technology, from our disparate past to our promising future, we'll take you inside Asian America in every issue. The hottest writers. The timeliest topics. Stunning design and photography. Get them all, six times a year, direct to your door.

GET A FREE PREVIEW COPY OF A. MAGAZINE, AND START YOUR NO-OBLIGATION TRIAL SUBSCRIPTION! USE THE COUPON BELOW OR CALL 1-800-346-0085 X 477 AND MENTION CODE MNB961.

If after getting your free copy, you don't like what you read, simply call us toll-free, or write "cancel" on your invoice and you'll owe absolutely nothing — the free issue is yours to keep. Otherwise, you'll receive six more issues of A. Magazine — a full year — for the low rate of $11 — 25% less than the regular subscription rate, and 38% lower than the newsstand price

"A. Magazine captures the life and times of Asian America, and gives them what they want — widely acclaimed editorial covering trends, leaders, culture, and style."
— *Inside Media* magazine.

Please send me a complimentary copy of A. Magazine and begin my no-obligation trial subscription at the special discount rate of $11 for six issues. If I do not like my sample copy, I can cancel my subscription when I get the invoice and will owe nothing. The free issue is mine to keep.

NAME _____

ADDRESS _____

CITY _____ STATE ____ ZIP ____

PHONE _____

O check enclosed
O bill me
O visa
O mastercard

CHARGE NO. _____ EXP. DATE ____

Mail to: A. Magazine / 270 Lafayette St. Suite 400 / NY, NY 10012

WHAT'S AVAILABLE:

- Over 2,600 Company Profiles
- Stock Quotes
- Stock Charts
- SEC Documents
- Quarterly Earnings
- Business Week in Review

- 10,000 Company Capsules
- IPO Documents
- Over 2,000 Corporate Web Sites
- 500 Sites with Job Opportunities
- Special Features
- Maps of Company Headquarters

WHO'S USING IT:

- Investors
- Job Seekers
- Brokers
- Professors

- Sales Executives
- Journalists
- Librarians
- Students

- Corporate Executives
- Competitive Intelligence Analysts
- Investment Bankers
- Market Researchers

WWW.HOOVERS.COM

Hoover's, Inc. • 1033 La Posada Drive, Suite 250 • Austin, Texas 78752
Phone 512-374-4500 • Fax 512-454-9401 • e-mail info@hoovers.com